The Best Tips from
25 Years of *Fine Woodworking*

TABLESAW

METHODS OF WORK

EDITED AND
ILLUSTRATED BY
JIM RICHEY

The Taunton Press

Publisher: Jim Childs
Associate Publisher: Helen Albert
Associate Editor: Strother Purdy
Copy Editor: Suzanne Noel
Indexer: Harriet Hodges
Art Director: Paula Schlosser
Cover and Interior Designer: Carol Singer
Layout Artist: Kathe Donovan
Illustrator: Jim Richey

FINE WOODWORKING MAGAZINE
Editor: Timothy D. Schreiner
Art Director: Bob Goodfellow
Managing Editor: Anatole Burkin
Associate Editors: William Duckworth, Matthew Teague,
  Asa Christiana
Copy/Production Editor: Thomas McKenna
Associate Art Director: Michael Pekovich

ABOUT YOUR SAFETY
Working with wood is inherently dangerous. Using hand or power tools improperly or ignoring standard safety practices can lead to permanent injury or even death. Don't try to perform operations you learn about here (or elsewhere) unless you're certain they are safe for you. If something about an operation doesn't feel right, don't do it. Look for another way. We want you to enjoy the craft, so please keep safety foremost in your mind whenever you're working with wood.

BOOKS & VIDEOS

for fellow enthusiasts

Printed in the United States of America
10 9 8 7 6 5 4 3 2 1

The Taunton Press, Inc.,
63 South Main Street, PO Box 5506,
Newtown, CT 06470-5506
e-mail: tp@taunton.com

Distributed by Publishers Group West

Library of Congress Cataloging-in-Publication Data
Tablesaw : methods of work / edited and illustrated by Jim Richey.
       p.   cm.
    "The best tips from 25 years of Fine woodworking."
    ISBN 1-56158-367-7
       1. Circular saw. 2. Woodwork. I. Richey, Jim. II. Fine woodworking.
    TT186.T33   2000
    684'.083—dc21   00-041156

ACKNOWLEDGMENTS

M AKING GOOD MAGAZINE COLUMNS and books is not a solitary endeavor—it requires collaboration of the finest kind. Twenty-some years ago John Kelsey took a chance on me—thanks, John. My deepest gratitude goes to the magazine staff members I've worked with over the years: Rick Mastelli, Jim Cummins, Jim Boesel, Alec Waters and Bill Duckworth. These guys did most of the hard work and didn't get much of the credit. I'd like also to recognize art directors Roland Wolf and Bob Goodfellow for their gentle and perceptive coaching. I am also most grateful for Strother Purdy's help and support in putting together this series of books.

But most importantly, I would like to thank the hundreds of woodworkers whose creative ideas and clever tricks are represented here. We couldn't have done it without you.

CONTENTS

INTRODUCTION

 I KNOW THE EXACT DATE I became a real woodworker—October 27, 1969. That was the day my wife gave me a tablesaw as a present for my 25th birthday. It was a belt-driven Sears Craftsman with an 8-in. blade. I proudly planted it in the middle of my one-car garage and began outfitting my modest little workshop around it.

Although I now have a little bigger and fancier tool, nothing much has changed: The tablesaw remains the heart of my workshop. And so it is for most woodworkers, professional and amateur alike. Our projects start on the tablesaw and return there time and again during the construction.

The tablesaw is truly a universal tool. It not only excels at ripping (its unrivaled specialty), but it also crosscuts, dadoes, shapes, miters, and grooves. Equipped with shopmade jigs and fixtures, it makes coved trim, tapered legs, finger-jointed boxes, and about any thing else you can think up.

There's something about the directness and simplicity of the tablesaw that inspires creative solutions in woodworkers. It just sits there—a cast-iron table, two tracks and a blade—ready and willing to solve your particular problem.

And that is what this book is all about—solutions. We've sifted through 25 years' worth of tablesaw tips from the Methods of Work and Q&A columns of *Fine Woodworking* magazine and collected the best here in one book. You will learn how to set up your saw, build guards and safety devices, make safer switches, build jigs and fixtures of every kind, and much more. There are, in fact, more tablesaw ideas here than you can shake a push stick at.

In short, you know that the tablesaw is your best shop buddy. Treat your buddy to this book.

Chapter 1

SETUP
&
MAINTENANCE

Heart of the Shop: Tablesaw or Radial-Arm Saw?

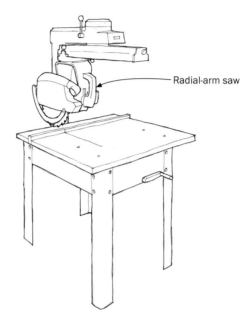

Radial-arm saw

THERE ARE COMPELLING REASONS to choose a tablesaw over a radial-arm saw. Although both machines can rip, crosscut and make angled cuts, the tablesaw is far superior in safety, accuracy and versatility.

The radial-arm saw is comparatively unsafe because its blade rotates in the direction of the cut. This causes the blade to try to pull itself toward you when you crosscut. Similarly, when you rip, the wood wants to self-feed. In both cases, you must simultaneously push and pull. Failure to balance these opposing actions can lead to disaster.

By way of contrast, the blade of a tablesaw rotates against the direction of the cut, so only pushing is required, which gives you far greater control.

As for accuracy, radial-arm saws can be set up to cut straight and square, but they are notorious for not holding true. Apparently, there's too much torque on too many movable parts. For this reason, the skilled woodworkers I know use their radial-arm saws exclusively for crosscutting rough lumber to approximate length, which is an operation that requires no accuracy whatsoever.

Tablesaws will dependably maintain their alignment and accuracy, and a well set-up tablesaw—with outfeed and side extension tables and a good rip fence—is versatile. My 10-in. tablesaw, outfitted with a standard Biesemeyer fence, will rip material up to 52 in. wide. Most radial-arm saws have half that capacity, or less. Crosscut capacity is generally about the same for the two machines, particularly if you make or buy a sliding crosscut box for your tablesaw. As for versatility, the tablesaw can also perform operations, such as cove cutting and tenoning, which are dangerous or impossible on a radial-arm saw.

—PETER KORN, *West Rockport, Maine,*
from a question by Robyn E. Tyler, Baton Rouge, La.

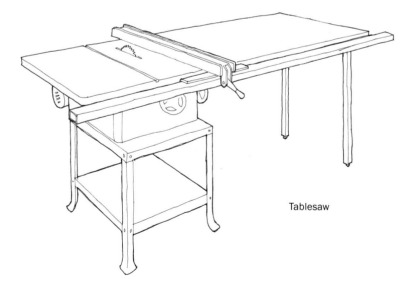

Tablesaw

Truing a Tablesaw Top

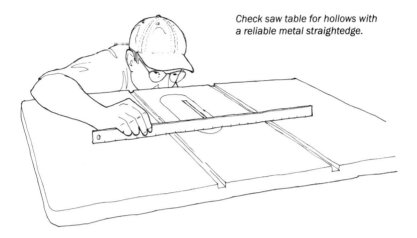

Check saw table for hollows with a reliable metal straightedge.

A COMMON PROBLEM FOUND IN older tablesaws is a top that is warped, leaving a slight hollow or concave spot in the middle of the table. If your saw has this problem, check the following points thoroughly and consider your alternatives before you take it to a machine shop to be milled.

First, make sure you have a reliable straightedge. Check it against another straightedge or a surface you know to be truly flat. Before measuring for levelness, make sure the throat plate isn't projecting above the saw top and lifting the straightedge. Also, check to see that the top's wing tables are not canted. If they angle up, they could be contributing to the hollow you detect. Loosen the screws that hold the tables and shim as necessary.

Set the blade square to the table and try both ripping and crosscutting. If the hollow in your top is concentrated near the blade, it will have a negligible impact on all but the narrowest pieces you rip and hardly any effect on crosscutting accuracy. If you do decide you can't live with the hollowness of your saw top, find a machine shop that has a Blanchard grinder. This type of machine can surface large areas very quickly, and the majority of the cost will be for set-up time. I had my 40-in. by 32-in. bandsaw table reground for $85. Of course, you'll have to remove the table from the saw before taking it to the shop.

—RICH PREISS, *Charlotte, N.C.,*
from a question by Eric Speth, St. Mary's City, Md.

Drilling a Saw Table

MANY WOODWORKERS HESITATE TO drill and tap into the surface of their tablesaw to mount jigs and fences because they are concerned about making the saw unsafe or reducing its resale value. Personally, I wouldn't hesitate to drill and tap my tablesaw surface. But the effectiveness of a jig will be only as good as the thought that precedes it. This also holds true for its safety. You don't want to reduce or restrict the basic effectiveness of your saw just for the sake of an add-on function. Be sure to mark out, drill and tap carefully so that you don't disfigure the table surface or make more holes than necessary. Check all your underside clearances carefully in advance to avoid drilling into or too close to the table ribs. Consider designing your jigs so that they can fasten to a common mounting plate instead of drilling separate holes for each jig. Though resale value is a consideration worth noting, I've seen many used saws with cleanly-tapped holes from production jigging retain their full resale potential.

—RICH PREISS, *Charlotte, N.C.,*
from a question by Dan Beatty, Louisville, Ky.

Wax vs. Talc for Cast Iron

R ECENTLY I READ THE OWNER'S manual for a Taiwanese tablesaw that specifically stated "do not use wax" to protect the surface and instead suggested using talc. Having been a longtime advocate of using paraffin wax for protecting and making cast-iron machine surfaces slicker, I was puzzled by the Taiwanese company's recommendation. I contacted the company's service manager, who told me that sprinkling on talc, or talcum powder, and then brushing it off will fill the pores in cast iron and keep surfaces dry, rust free and slick, albeit for a short time. He did not know where this procedure originated. He said that the company warned against wax because of the fear that transferring oily or waxy substances to the workpiece may hamper subsequent finishing operations.

In my opinion, hard wax still provides excellent lubrication and protection for cast-iron surfaces, no matter who manufactures the machine. The most important aspect of applying the wax, however, is buffing off the excess 10 or 15 minutes after application (use plenty of elbow grease and a clean rag). And occasionally clean the entire surface with a mild solvent, such as mineral spirits or VM&P naphtha. Repeated applications where excess wax isn't rubbed off will build up on the metal, and the wax may eventually transfer to anything that touches the surface.

The issue of oily or waxy transfer is important, but consider this: Most wood will be planed, scraped or sanded extensively before finish is applied. Any wax buildup on the workpiece would be on the surface and would be removed before finishing. If you normally edge-join boards directly off the jointer, or if you wax the soles of your handplanes, make sure you use either surface to some degree prior to taking your final passes. This way, you wear off the bulk of the wax, minimizing the possibility that wax will transfer to the edge and later affect the integrity of your glue joint.

—RICH PREISS, *Charlotte, N.C.,*
from a question by Marshall G. Baldwin, Westport, Conn.

Securing Machines with Adhesive

THE USUAL SOLUTION FOR securing benches and machines is to bolt them to the workshop floor. An alternative to this is to glue the equipment to the floor with a high-quality panel-and-construction adhesive. After you have positioned your machines, level them with small wooden shims. Then use a caulking gun to run a bead around the base of the equipment, and smooth the bead quickly with your finger. When the adhesive cures, it becomes very durable and hard. The benches won't rock when you are working, and the machines won't creep. If you decide to relocate a machine in the future, you can simply remove the adhesive with a chisel.

—RICHARD H. DORN, *Oelwein, Iowa*

Dampening Noisy Sheet-Metal Machinery Stands

Glue plywood strip
to stand to deaden
vibration.

Hᴇʀᴇ'ѕ ʜᴏᴡ ᴛᴏ ǫᴜɪᴇᴛ ᴀ ɴᴏɪѕʏ ᴍᴀᴄʜɪɴᴇ on a sheet-metal
stand—the one that seems to rumble and boom to a distracting
degree. First make sure all the fasteners on the machine are tight. Then
check to make sure the machine is sitting squarely on the floor. If a
shim or two doesn't solve the problem, I would then turn my attention to the sheet-metal stand. While the machine is idling, feel the
sides of the stand and press in on different places to see if there are
any changes in the sound. If you feel one of the panels vibrating more
than the others, put a wood stiffener on it. To do this, cut a couple of
3-in.-wide (or wider) strips of plywood, and coat one side of each
with construction adhesive. Now squish them in place on the inside of
the stand wherever the panel was vibrating (space permitting). Tape
the strip in place or wedge with sticks as necessary, and let the adhesive dry for about a day. This technique usually does the job for me.

—Rᴏʙᴇʀᴛ Vᴀᴜɢʜᴀɴ, *Roanoke, Va.,*
from a question by Herbert Weiner, Sarasota, Fla.

Correcting Sears Tablesaw Pulley Problems

SOME OLDER SEARS 10-IN. TABLESAWS use the weight of the drive motor to tension the belt that drives the blade. This system works well when it is new and properly adjusted. However, when the system is worn or poorly adjusted, the motor and drive pulley will cant, causing the belt to climb the edge of the pulley, resulting in noticeable vibration and excessive belt wear. If your saw exhibits this problem, here are some suggestions.

First, determine if the position of the motor slips because the bolts that attach the motor to its mounting plate loosen. If that is the case, I would suggest fitting lock washers under the nuts and star-type (external tooth) washers between the mounting plate and the motor itself. Most hardware stores carry these star washers as a specialty item in a bolt or fastener display. Is the bracket that attaches the mounting plate to the tablesaw frame worn or bent? If it is worn and sloppy, you may be able to rebuild it by drilling out the hole for the bolt or pin that hinges it and using a larger bolt or pin. If the bracket is bent or broken, you can probably order a new one from Sears.

Another possible remedy would be to bolt the motor on at a slight angle, away from the direction of sag. This should cause the motor and its pulley to be straight when belt tension is applied. If all else fails, you might try bolting a piece of angle iron to the motor bracket under the frame to keep the motor steady.

—MARK DUGINSKE, *Wausau, Wisc.,*
from a question by Hugh L. Pryor, Walnut Creek, Calif.

How Much Sawblade Runout Can You Live With?

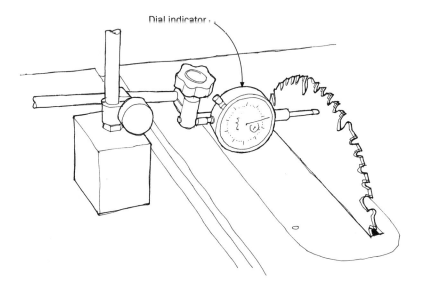

Dial indicator

IF YOU HAVE CHRONIC CUTTING PROBLEMS on your tablesaw one of the first things you should check is the amount of runout on the blade. Just borrow a dial indicator with a magnetic base, put the feeler against the blade and spin it to see the variation. Almost every blade will exhibit at least a small amount of runout. It is hard to say how much is too much, but runout of as little as 0.008 in. could have a small but noticeably negative effect on the smoothness of cut your saw produces. The runout may also increase the pressure required to feed stock through the blade.

Even the bodies of new sawblades are rarely flat, and hard use will quickly increase the amount of runout. On tablesaws, pinched stock between the table opening and the blade can cause blade warpage, as can bind and kickback.

It may be possible to reduce your runout. Start by rechecking the blade. Observe the dial indicator's needle as the sawblade is rotated. If the extremes of the reading are 180° apart, then the cause of the runout may be the arbor flange. Try changing the position of the blade on the arbor to see if it decreases the runout. If the variation goes in and out all around the blade, then the body of the blade is most likely warped, which is the probable source of your runout.

My experience with blade problems over the years has ultimately revealed one common denominator—age. I have found that no matter how well the blade has been sharpened, older sawblades (some of mine are 8 to 15 years old) just won't cut the way they used to. The only consistent solution is to replace the blade. Even though an old blade may look great hanging on the wall and have plenty of sharpenable carbide remaining on the tips, it still isn't worth keeping if it's not cutting satisfactorily after sharpening. The skill and technology required to make an old blade flat again is not worth the expense to me when compared to the cost of a new blade.

—ROBERT VAUGHAN, *Roanoke, Va.,*
from a question by Graham Laird, Ashstead, Surrey, England

Eliminating Saw Buzz

W HEN RIPPING THICKER HARDWOODS, some sawblades will occasionally "buzz" in the kerf, leaving a slight roughness, burn or both. The first thing I would try to eliminate this problem is installing blade stabilizers. Blade stabilizers will improve the performance of any sawblade. They minimize the vibration by stiffening the blade enough to help keep each tooth directly in line with every tooth on the blade. This results in a truer-running blade that stays sharp longer and cuts smoother. If you purchase stabilizers, be sure they are true; crooked stabilizers will aggravate any runout or wobble problems. I find machined steel stabilizers or sawblade blanks sold by saw shops to be excellent; I haven't had good results with cast-aluminum stabilizers.

Even without stabilizers, though, sawblades should not buzz in the kerf. A blade that does this has a problem with plate tension and should be taken to a qualified saw service. When the blade cuts, friction heats the rim, expanding the steel toward the center of the blade. This is like trying to scrunch too much steel into a small area, causing the blade to buzz or wobble.

Cutting with an excessively high feed rate, which prevents the blade from clearing chips fast enough and thus causes heat buildup, amplifies the problems with improperly tensioned blades.

—DAVID P. SNOOK, *Salem, Ore.,*
from a question by Tim McCarthy, Oak Harbor, Wash.

Blade Stabilizers: Useful Tool or Gimmick?

SOME WOODWORKERS BUY A pair of blade stabilizers and then expect miracles from them—like elimination of blade noise. Stabilizers are intended to keep thin blades from wobbling at high rpms, not to cut down on noise. Before the age of carbide-tipped blades, saw makers relied on steel blades that were tempered to a Rockwell hardness of 46 to 48, anything over 48 being too brittle for a sawblade. These blades were then tensioned and flattened by highly skilled saw smiths using an assortment of hammers and straightedges to ensure accuracy when the blade was run. Most blade manufacturers today, because of the shortage of saw smiths and the high cost of their labor, use saw plates with hardness ratings of 36 to 40, which are tensioned and flattened by machines. These softer blades tend to bend easier than harder ones. Stabilizing collars might keep these softer blades straighter on the arbor and result in less noise, because a true-running blade cuts through the air more cleanly. So, are stabilizers gimmicks? All I can say is that they may help sometimes, but more often, they don't.

If what you are after is a reduction in noise, here are a couple of other ideas. If the blade in question has expansion slots with holes at the bottom, have a saw shop plug them with copper. That might quiet things down. Also, you might put some type of deflector on the blade guard to change the airflow. This could be a considerable noise factor, considering the blade is probably turning about 3,450 rpm.

—MARSHALL BURNS, *Fall River, Mass.,*
from a question by Bob Maxwell, Washington, D.C.

Sawblade Stabilizers

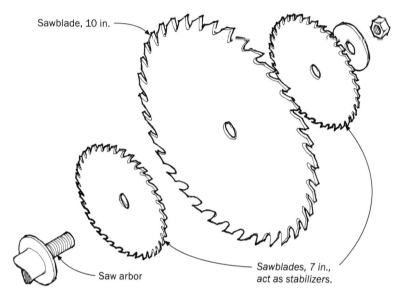

Sawblade, 10 in.

Saw arbor

Sawblades, 7 in.,
act as stabilizers.

WHEN I BEGAN EXPERIENCING some blade wobble and vibration problems on my tablesaw, I looked into but rejected a set of expensive mail-order blade stabilizers. Later, I noticed a couple of used 7-in. circular sawblades hanging around the shop waiting to be sharpened. I sandwiched my 10-in. tablesaw blade between the two smaller blades to act as a stabilizer. The arrangement solved my blade wobble and vibration problems. I'm sure that smaller-diameter blades, which would allow for a greater cutting depth, would also work effectively.

—LES BARNA, *Indialantic, Fla.*

Silencing Carbide Sawblades

IF YOUR CARBIDE SAW BLADE IS NOISY, here are a few suggestions. Keep in mind, though, that there can be many reasons for noisy carbide blades, and you may have to consult a professional saw technician to solve your problem. Blades commonly make two types of noise. One is generally referred to as whistling, the other as ringing or screaming.

Several things can cause whistling. If several blades whistle on the same machine, the problem could be the guard. Think of the sawblade as a fan, with each tooth acting as a fan blade. If you put a fan that moves air into a housing, you create a siren. Putting a sawblade onto a machine with a guard can create the same effect. In order to change the airflow, either the guard or the blade must be altered. Turning the guard slightly can sometimes be enough to make a difference. Drilling holes in the guard or shortening or lengthening it can also make a difference, but unless you know quite a lot about air flows, you'd be working on a trial-and-error basis and could increase the problem rather than correct it.

If the blade itself is a problem, you'd probably need to have it checked by a professional saw serviceman. The saw gullet depth could be incorrect. The angle of the heel relief behind the carbide tips could be incorrect or at the wrong height in relation to the tip. Radial or tangential side clearance of the carbide might be the problem. Sometimes you can quiet a blade by filling the expansion slots or holes in the blade with lead solder, copper, brass, resin or silicone plugs. Be careful that the finished plug is flush with or thinner than the saw plate itself.

A screaming blade has a much more shrill and penetrating sound than a whistling blade. If there are tight spots in the steel—places where the molecules are closer together than in other areas in the saw plate—the blade will be out of balance when it spins, and this will cause it to oscillate or vibrate in the same way a ringing bell does. This problem must be corrected by a properly equipped saw-service shop, with personnel skilled in hammering blades to tension or stress-relieve the metal.

—DAVID SNOOK, *Salem, Ore.,*
from a question by Martin F. Mueller, Chicago, Ill.

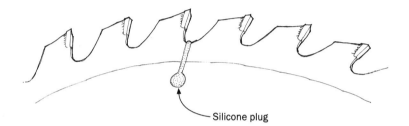

Silicone plug

Sawblade Speeds

IF YOU ARE THINKING ABOUT changing out your saw motor or saw pulleys to increase the rpm of the blade I'd exercise some caution. As you can see from the table below, the larger the blade, the slower the recommended rpm. Most larger blades don't have a blade body that can run at the high rpm of 6,000 (which is also 100 revolutions per second) without experiencing metal fatigue and deformation, and they also tend to deviate or flutter at that speed. A faulty blade could even fly apart.

All blades are tensioned to run at a given rpm, and they will likely wobble or run out if they're run at a substantially different speed. Only the better-quality blades are hand-tensioned in the first place, so finding one will probably involve paying a bit extra. My firm, Winchester, hand-tensions its sawblades to run as fast as 6,500 rpm. As a general rule, 10,000 sfm (surface feet per minute) is the desirable speed at which to run a sawblade. Sfm is a measure of the distance a saw tooth will travel in a straight line in one minute. In special applications, a different speed can be used. Most people, however, shoot for 10,000 sfm for general usage, and the chart gives these figures. In the general shop, all blades should run at the speed recommended in the chart, but a coarse-tooth ripping blade can run 10% to 15% slower.

Blade diameter	Rpm
6 in.	6,622
8 in.	4,830
10 in.	3,831
12 in.	3,184
14 in.	2,732
16 in.	2,398
18 in.	2,123

Recommended sawblade speeds (equal to 10,000 sfm).

—TOM MILLER, *from a question by Mike Conner, Juneau, Alaska*

Blade Speed for 10-In. Tablesaw

THERE'S NO CONSENSUS ON the optimum blade speed for a 10-in. tablesaw. Most used to run at about 4,000 rpm. Delta's contractor's saws ran at that speed for years. Things change. They now run at 3,450 rpm. Delta says that this does not adversely affect cutting performance but increases the torque. The only potential problem I see is that a smaller motor pulley means a sharper bend for a V-belt. With a standard V-belt, this could introduce vibration or lead to premature failure. A cogged V-belt should be able to handle the tighter radius without any problems. The higher the speed, the greater the strain on the bearings and the sooner they'll need to be replaced. Blades running at high speeds tend to throw sawdust all over the place, including your face, as you're cutting. And high blade speed will lead to heat buildup at the blade tips. The bottom line? Keep your blade speed under 4,000 rpm, and use a good blade with the correct tooth configuration.

—ROBERT VAUGHAN, *Roanoke, Va., from a question by Bob Ricker, Chicago, Ill.*

Lubricating Sawblades with a Nonstick Spray

SAWBLADES WILL STAY CLEAN longer and clean up faster next time if sprayed with a kitchen nonstick product such as PAM. After spraying, hold a piece of cardboard over the blade to catch the mist thrown off, while sawing a scrap or two to clear the excess oil from the blade before you use it on good stock.

—DAVID L. WISELEY, *Waters, Mich.*

Smaller Blades for More Power

I F YOU RUN A SMALLER BLADE on a tablesaw, for example a 9-in. blade on a 10-in. tablesaw, it will increase power of the blade simply because of the law of mechanical advantage. The torque is greater as you approach the center of the blade. The speed of the blade may seem higher because the blade will not bog down so much in heavy cuts. Actually, the speed of the blade at the teeth is slower than with a 10-in. blade, but this doesn't cause problems. Another way to seemingly increase power is to change pulley sizes to slow the saw down, but my favorite method is to go to a blade with fewer teeth, especially when ripping. A thin-kerf blade also uses less power, because it's removing less wood.

—JIM CUMMINS, *from a question by H. Duane Bartlett, Detroit, Mich.*

Cleaning Sawblades with Oven Cleaner

T O CLEAN THE GUMMY buildup on sawblades, spray the blade with oven cleaner. I use the foaming type that contains 4% lye. Let the sprayed blade stand a while until the gummy deposit lifts, then rinse under the tap. Oven cleaner is powerful, caustic stuff, so observe the warnings on the label. Do not use on aluminum tools.

—G.V. MUMFORD, *Ventura, Calif.*

Tablesaw-Blade Runout: How Much is Too Much?

I AM OFTEN ASKED ABOUT the standards for blade runout on a tablesaw. A typical question is "is a blade runout of 0.011 in. on a Sears 10-in. tablesaw excessive?" My first reaction is yes, I would become suspect if my saw had an 0.011-in. blade runout. But the manufacturer of Sears's tablesaws, Emerson Electric Co., considers runout of as much as 0.015 in. to be "normal and within our production standards."

Part of the problem is that there are no industrywide standards for woodworking-machine production, either in this country or abroad. It seems that the consumer market, by its acceptance or rejection of the product, determines whether a manufacturer's standards are "close enough."

—RICHARD PREISS, *Charlotte, N.C.,*
from a question by Michael Murray, Xenia, Ohio

Cleaning Sawblades with Baking Soda

A FTER RUNNING OUT OF commercial pitch remover to clean my sawblades, I gathered some suggestions for home remedies from a newsgroup on the Internet (rec.woodworking). I tried almost all the suggestions I received. One of the most effective is to place the blade in an old cake pan, sprinkle baking soda on it and add a teapot full of boiling water. It works amazingly well.

Dark green, professional 409 glass cleaner and automotive carburetor cleaners both remove heavily burned pitch from router bits and sawblades, and they're much less expensive than commercial pitch removers.

—MIKE VINCENT, *Littleton, Colo.*

Shop Uses for a Pizza Pan

A 12-IN.-DIA. PIZZA PAN can be quite handy around the shop. Use it as a tub to clean your circular sawblades, to keep small parts from rolling off the bench and, with a sheet of nonslip rubber in the bottom, as a basin for sharpening with Japanese waterstones.

—MIKE HIPPS, *Minneapolis, Minn.*

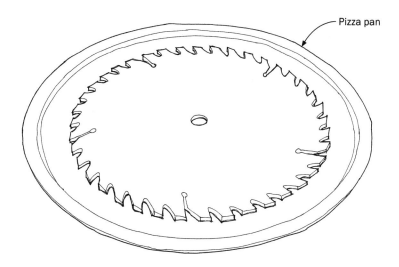

Pizza pan

Wavering and Binding Tablesaw Cuts

I F, WHEN RIPPING LONG STOCK, your tablesaw cuts a wavering, crooked line for a foot or two, and then binds in the kerf, my suspicions would first center on the stock. Each time that "binding" problem happens, look hard at the stock to see if it's twisted. Just a small amount of twist over the length of the plank, or trying to saw a plank with the concave curve next to the fence, will bring the best of saws to a roaring halt. What's more, the chance that the rip fence is toeing in a little makes sawing long planks on a tablesaw a chancy thing for anyone working alone. Long pieces are best sawn with a helper ready to jam a screwdriver in a closing kerf and help steer the stick. Even with a roller supporting the end of a stick you can still have this binding problem. If the roller is slightly askew of the plank's line of travel, the plank will slip sideways and bind. Grain tension can skew the plank, too, but you'd spot that problem quickly enough when the kerf started closing on you.

The saw itself is likely not at fault, but I'd definitely check the fence for misalignment. If the fence opens just a hair from being parallel to the back of the sawblade, that's okay. But a toe-in is a definite fault and must be corrected.

If these remedies don't work you can finish the cut with a bandsaw or a portable circular saw. Using a portable circular saw with a guide makes sawing long lengths a breeze.

If you experience similar binding problems with plywood I'd suspect that your feed is too fast, the sawblade is too high or your rip fence has unnoticed toe-in. Improperly sharpened saws, either hand or power, with teeth longer on one side than on the other (or dull on one side) can also get you into binding problems.

All of these problems can ruin your day and keep you from doing a proper sawing job. Worse yet, they're enough to drive you nuts because they're often almost imperceptible.

—HAROLD "DYNAMITE" PAYSON, *South Thomaston, Maine, from a question by J. J. Gibbens, Lafayette, La.*

More Solutions for Wavering and Binding

L ET ME ADD A COUPLE OF THINGS to Harold Payson's advice for curing wavering and binding. First make sure your saw is not underpowered. You need at least a 1½-hp motor on a 10-in. tablesaw to rip thick materials. Second, make sure your blade is not dull and that you are not trying to rip with a combination blade instead of a blade designed for ripping. Or, maybe you're using a rip blade, but one with too many teeth. What happens with a dull or incorrect blade—especially with an underpowered saw—is that each tooth doesn't have the power behind it to take a full cut. Instead, the blade bogs down and the teeth skid, producing friction and heat. This can actually cause the disc of the blade to buckle slightly from expansion, at which point cutting becomes impossible. When the blade cools off, it flattens out again. I saw this happen once years ago when cutting Plexiglas with an 8-in. plywood blade—the blade began first to bind, then to wander, then it stalled. The blade disc was warped almost an inch out of true. Fifteen minutes later, it was flat again. I suspect that the same thing happens with wood, because the symptoms of a deteriorating cut are the same, even when the kerf appears to be open.

You won't be sorry if you treat yourself to a 10-tooth ripping blade from a good saw shop. I bought one about eight years ago from Winchester (2633 Paper Mill Rd., Winchester, VA 22601) for $45. The same blade costs about $65 today, but that's inconsequential when you average out the cost over the anticipated life of the blade. Also, it will pay for itself in the wood you don't ruin. I still think, though, that you'll need the larger motor as well. As a last thought, my saw would barely cut a 2x4 when at the end of a 50-ft. extension cord; plug your saw directly into a wall or floor outlet if you can.

—JIM CUMMINS, *from a question by J. J. Gibbens, Lafayette, La.*

Trouble with a Tablesaw's Cut

WHEN RIPPING WITH SOME TABLESAWS, the material may move away from the fence just beyond the blade on the outfeed side. This problem is not only disturbing but can also result in dangerous kickback.

There are a number of things that can cause this problem. First of all, the rip fence needs to be perfectly straight. As simple as this sounds, I have seen many saw fences come right out of the manufacturer's box and not be straight. The best way to straighten a crooked fence is to bolt an auxiliary wood (preferably plywood) fence to it. Shims are used to keep the new straight fence from assuming the shape of the crooked one when it's bolted on. You can punch out your own shims from cardboard or from aluminum-can stock, and insert them between the auxiliary and stock fences. Also, you can use the shims to square the fence to the saw table.

Next, check for blade misalignment, also called "heeling." Follow the directions that came with your saw or in a tablesaw-maintenance book to align the blade and saw table properly. Don't mistakenly assume that you can just set the rip fence parallel to the saw table's miter slot: The slot and sawblade may not be parallel. Blade misalignment is common and is most likely the cause of the problem. Some people prefer to have the fence angled very slightly so that the distance between the fence and blade is minutely greater (between $\frac{1}{64}$ in. and $\frac{1}{32}$ in.) at the back of the blade.

Another condition that can cause this problem is not related to the tablesaw at all. The wood may be releasing tension and distorting as a result of being cut. This can cause the wood between the rip fence and the blade to bow away from the fence. If this is what's occurring, it's best to fit the saw with a kerf splitter—a special thin, curved bar that's mounted behind the blade to keep the saw kerf from closing up and pinching the blade. However, if internal tension in the wood is the problem, the opposite situation may also arise: The two pieces may spread apart after being cut. The spreading can cause the portion of the workpiece between the fence and blade to bind against the blade, generating a kickback. For this reason, Europeans prefer to use a short fence for ripping, which only reaches as far as the back of the blade, providing clearance when cutting solid wood.

—MARK DUGINSKE, *Wausau, Wisc.*,
from a question by Ronald D. Frey, Clay, N.Y.

Reducing Saw Burns on Maple

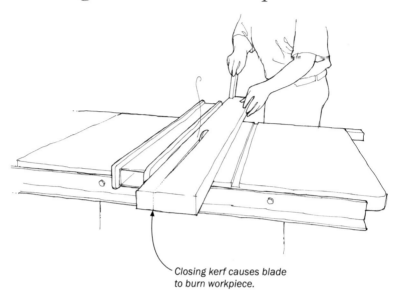

Closing kerf causes blade
to burn workpiece.

HARD MAPLE SEEMS TO BURN EASIER than most other woods—especially when ripping rather than when crosscutting. Here are some suggestions for avoiding this problem: Best results can be achieved with either a 24-tooth carbide rip blade or a 40-tooth combination blade. Your saw must have sufficient power to sustain full-blade speed at a moderate feed rate. If the saw drags, burning can result. Carbide tips that have been ground too often can reduce kerf clearance and generate enough heat to burn hardwoods. Also, keep your blades clean, especially if you cut softwoods with the same saw. Soap, warm water and a toothbrush can remove the residue that accumulates behind carbide teeth or on the blade side, generating additional friction.

Very often when ripping maple—especially thick material that's not straight-grained or dry—the kerf tends to close back around the blade.

The resulting pinch will cause enough friction to blacken one or both edges. The splitter that came with your saw will help keep the pieces separated, or you could wedge the kerf open. If you find the burning occurs more on the keeper piece next to the fence than on the cutoff, check the parallel alignment of the rip fence. A fence that toes toward the blade even slightly can cause the blade to burn hard material.

When cutting to length, I prefer a 50-tooth carbide combination blade, but I've had good luck with "fine" steel crosscut blades. Steer clear of hollow-ground blades that have no set—they overheat too quickly. Burn during crosscutting most often occurs for one of three reasons: dull or misshapen teeth, too slow a feed rate, or the fact that the rear section of the blade is rubbing against the hard end grain after the cut is made. To prevent this kind of rubbing, keep straight-ahead pressure on the material as you cut.

—RICH PREISS, *Charlotte, N.C.,*
from a question by John Sampson, San Juan, Puerto Rico

Lubricating Tablesaw Adjustment Gears

T O LUBRICATE TIGHT, BINDING ADJUSTING GEARS in a tablesaw, first vacuum and then brush the mechanism with a nylon parts-cleaning brush. Then spray the gears with a chain lube such as Whitmore's Open Chain Lubricant or PJ-1 Heavy Duty Chain Lube. These slippery-film lubricants are well adapted to the dusty environment under the saw's table. An occasional application will provide continued smooth adjustment action, even when cutting abrasive materials like fiberboard or Masonite.

—JOHN GREW-SHERIDAN, *San Francisco, Calif.*

Avoiding Burned Bevels

W HEN CUTTING BEVELED PANELS on a tablesaw, saw burns can be a problem. The best way to minimize burns is to use a new or recently sharpened carbide blade—a 60- to 80-tooth ATB (alternate top bevel) would be fine—and be sure that the sides of the blade are clean. Remove any gummy deposits with oven cleaner. With the panel facedown on the tablesaw, make a shallow cut on all four sides to outline the raised panel area and mark the top of the bevel. The bevel cut intersecting with this cut frees the waste. After adjusting the saw fence and setting the blade at the proper angle, cut the beveled section. It might help to make a rough cut first to remove most of the waste, then make a light finishing cut. Push the wood briskly through the saw. The more you linger, the more likely you are to get burns. Depending on how big the panels are, it often helps to screw an extrahigh auxiliary fence to the regular metal saw fence to ensure that the stock is truly vertical when you saw the bevels. I find a cabinet scraper is the best way to clean up the surfaces. If you don't object to tool marks, you could try a shoulder rabbet plane.

SIMON WATTS, *San Francisco, Calif.,*
from a question by Mark Blieske, Winnipeg, Manitoba, Canada

Making Tablesaw Inserts with a Router

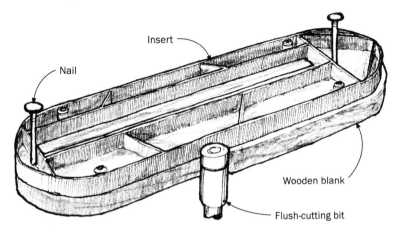

Insert

Nail

Wooden blank

Flush-cutting bit

D RILLING TWO NAIL-SIZED HOLES in your tablesaw insert lets you
tack the insert to a rough-cut blank and pattern-rout a replacement wooden insert that's exactly the size of the original. A flush-trim
bit with a ball-bearing pilot works best for the routing. Before you
start, thickness-plane the stock for the blanks to the exact depth of
your insert hole. I make up the inserts by the dozen and put in a new
one at each blade change.

—JEFFREY P. GYVING, *Point Arena, Calif.*

Prolonging the Life of an Old Tablesaw

TO KEEP A WORN TRUNNION on an old tablesaw working freely, try silicone spray, floor wax or "moly" lube, which is available in a dry powder. Keep the dust blown out with an air hose. If this doesn't help, the tilting gears are probably worn out. If the manufacturer doesn't carry the parts, try to locate a used saw and salvage the parts you need. Or possibly, a vocational school could cut the necessary gears.

—LELON TRAYLOR, *from a question by Mike Townsend, Canton, Mich.*

Oils for Lubricating Tablesaw Gears

I OFTEN RECOMMEND USING MACHINE oil to lubricate the gears and moving parts of tablesaws and other power tools. But machine oils are sometimes hard to find, and oil distributors recommend automobile engine oils instead. Machine oils are specifically formulated for lubricating machine parts. They cling to a surface without running off because they have a tackiness not found in engine oils. Some special lubricating oils used on die-stamping presses feel almost like thin molasses. Gun oil, available at sporting-goods stores, and sewing-machine oil are good machine oils. South Bend Lathe (400 W. Sample St., South Bend, IN 46623) sells machine oil in quarts, but a minimum order of $10 is required. McMaster Carr Supply Co. (P.O. Box 4355, Chicago, IL 60680) supplies machine oil in gallons.

—LELON TRAYLOR, *from a question by Melvyn J. Howe, St. Paul, Mo.*

Removable Toolbox for a Tablesaw

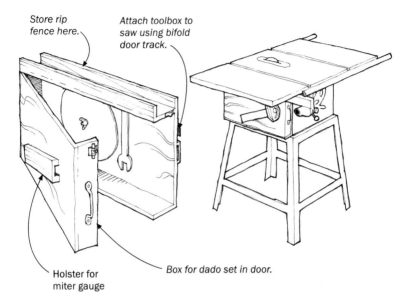

Store rip fence here.

Attach toolbox to saw using bifold door track.

Holster for miter gauge

Box for dado set in door.

I MADE THIS REMOVABLE TABLESAW toolbox for easy portability on construction jobs. The ¾-in. plywood box holds sawblades, a dado set, table inserts and so on. I added a channel to the top of the box to hold the rip fence when it's not needed. A hollow cleat on the side holds the miter gauge. I attached the box to the saw with a section of a used bifold door track so that I can slide the box off the saw.

—HARVEY W. BYLER, *Burton, Ohio*

Home for Tablesaw Accessories

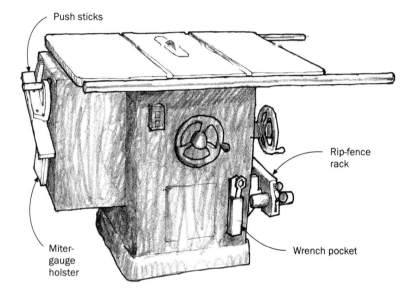

Push sticks

Rip-fence
rack

Miter-
gauge
holster

Wrench pocket

T HE LAST TIME I USED MY TABLESAW on a project that required
both crosscuts and rips, I couldn't find a place to park the rip
fence and miter gauge to keep them safely close at hand. Plus, the
blade-changing wrench was always lost in the shop clutter, and my
push sticks constantly wandered out of reach—just when I needed
them most.

To resolve these problems, I decided to make homes for all my
tablesaw attachments by building simple scrap-wood holsters and racks
at various places on the saw. The drawing illustrates the idea.

—FRED H. SIDES, *Mt. Kisco, N.Y.*

Utility Shelf for the Tablesaw

I FIND THAT A SHELF BUILT AROUND THE FRONT of my tablesaw base
is invaluable for keeping items (pencil, tape measure, miter gauge,
bench brush, push sticks, blade wrench) handy. I built the shelf from
¾-in. plywood, supported it with two steel shelf brackets and finished
it with scraps of molding around the edge.

—ROBERT E. BROWN, *Watertown, N.Y.*

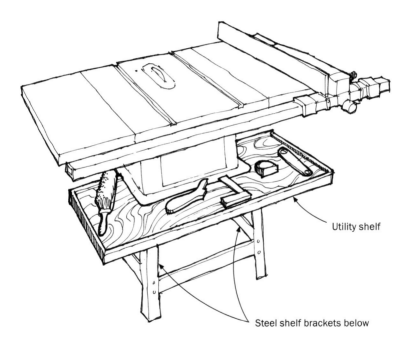

Utility shelf

Steel shelf brackets below

Improving Tablesaw Dust Collection

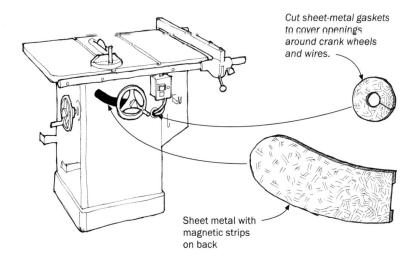

Cut sheet-metal gaskets to cover openings around crank wheels and wires.

Sheet metal with magnetic strips on back

I WASN'T GETTING ENOUGH SUCTION with my dust collector at the sawblade on my Delta Unisaw because of the large openings around the crank wheels and the switch wire. My solution was to seal the openings. I cut a scrap of sheet metal the same shape as the slot around the arbor-tilt wheel but ½ in. larger than the opening. I added some rubber magnetic strip (available at most craft-supply stores) to the outside edges so that I can remove the cover easily. I added sheet-metal gaskets to block other openings around the blade-height crank wheel and wire ports.

—TED ASOUSA, *Broomall, Pa.*

Tablesaw Light

F OR MANY YEARS, I used my tablesaw outside. I didn't realize how much I used the natural light flooding through the frame of the saw until I moved the saw into my newly completed garage and enclosed the sides to contain the sawdust. To replace the natural light I lost, I installed a clear Christmas-tree lightbulb inside the saw near the right front corner of the blade-insert opening. Then I wired the light directly to the saw switch.

I like to sight down the surface of the blade with one eye to align the blade with the pencil mark on the wood. That was impossible to do when the void below the top was in darkness. By unplugging the motor cord from the switch box and then turning the switch back on, I have all the light I need for changing the blade.

—DONALD SWITZER, *San Diego, Calif.*

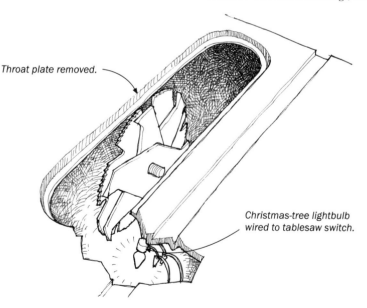

Throat plate removed.

Christmas-tree lightbulb
wired to tablesaw switch.

A Tablesaw Clamp

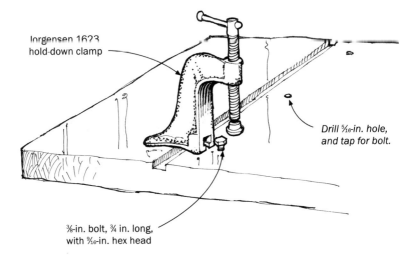

Jorgensen 1623
hold-down clamp

Drill ⁵⁄₁₆-in. hole,
and tap for bolt.

⅜-in. bolt, ¾ in. long,
with ⁹⁄₁₆-in. hex head

B ECAUSE SPACE HAS ALWAYS been a concern in my small shop, the
top of my tablesaw has often served second duty as a workbench.
I found that by securing removable Jorgensen model 1623 hold-down
clamps to the saw table, I could make the saw into a workbench without affecting its intended use. Four tapped holes in a saw table allow
for a surprisingly versatile choice of clamping positions. I also use the
holes to bolt a protective piece of plywood to the saw table for chisel
work, to attach a router table and to secure featherboards and other
tablesaw jigs and fixtures.

When locating the clamp's hole positions, be sure to avoid the cast
reinforcing ribs in the table's underside. Center-punch each hole location, and then drill with a sharp ⁵⁄₁₆-in. bit. When tapping the ⅜-in. bolt
threads, rotate the tap a half turn in, then back it out a quarter turn,
and so on. This action will break up the chips and keep the tap cutting

freely. Don't force the tap, and when you're done, chamfer the hole to keep any sharp edges from scratching your workpieces. Screw a ⅜-in. bolt with a ⁹⁄₁₆-in. hex head into the threaded hole. Leave the head of the bolt slightly above the table, so the slot in the clamp can be slid over it. The size of the slot just fits the head on the bolt and thus becomes a sort of wrench for tightening the bolt.

—STEVE ACKER, *Arlington, Tex.*

An American Tablesaw That Will Work in Europe

HERE'S SOME ADVICE FOR woodworkers who want to buy a tablesaw that will work both in the United States, where the electric system supplies 60 Hz, and in Germany where it is 50 Hz. The key fact is that you can run a 50-Hz motor on 60-Hz electricity, but you cannot do the reverse. In the United States, all manufacturers supply their saws with a 60-Hz motor. A U.S.-purchased saw will therefore not work on European 50-Hz electricity. However, almost any major manufacturer (Delta, Powermatic, etc.) will supply, on special order, a 230v, 50-Hz motor at an additional cost of $100 to $150 or so. While in the United States, the 50-Hz motor will run fine on 60-Hz electricity. When you ship the saw to Germany, just change the end of the power cord and the saw will work there also.

—RON ROCKOVICH, *Pittsburgh, Pa.,*
from a question by Werner Hinsken, Cary, N.C.

Scribing Accurate Kerf Lines
with Machinist's Dye

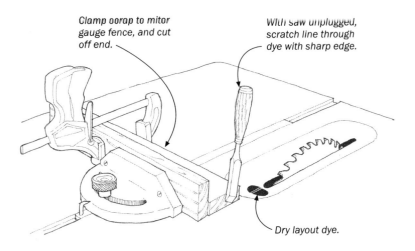

Clamp oorap to mitor
gauge fence, and cut
off end.

WItli saw unplugged,
scratch line through
dye with sharp edge.

Dry layout dye.

I HAVE IMPROVED THE SPEED and accuracy of my tablesaw cuts by
scribing precise, easy-to-read cut lines on the throat plate. To make
the lines, apply machinist's layout dye to a small area of the plate, and
let it dry. Clamp a piece of scrap to the miter gauge, and cut it off.
Using the freshly cut edge of the scrap as a guide, lightly scribe a line
in the dye. Repeat this operation on the right side of the blade to give
two lines. The dye makes the lines stand out, and it can be removed
with alcohol and the process repeated when the blade is changed.

—GLADDEN GRIGGS, *South Bend, Ind.*

Eliminating Runout in Modern Sawblade Manufacturing

M Y GOOD FRIEND TOM MILLER, owner of Winchester Carbide Saw, has stated, "Only the better-quality blades are hand-tensioned in the first place." He's absolutely correct, but he didn't go far enough. Hand tensioning, properly done, is an art. And there are very few fellows left who can actually hammer-tension to achieve a minimum of runout at a certain rpm. But hammer tensioning, at best, can't be consistent and can't produce two blades that perform exactly the same at a given rpm.

Here at Forrest Mfg. Co. we have a process that eliminates the runout that hammer tensioning can't, at any rpm. The plates for our blades are purchased thicker than final dimension. The supplier has roll-tensioned each plate, and the plate is "warped" or bellied like the bottom of an oil can. It is first ground perfectly flat, then ground to final thickness. The surface is checked with a straightedge, and any remaining undulations are pressed out.

The result is runout of not more than 0.001 in. (with a perfect arbor and collars). A dampener (not a stiffener) should be installed with the blade to kill harmonics from outside sources (motor, belts, etc.), so the blade will run true from 1 rpm to 6,500 rpm.

—WALLACE M. KUNKEL *for Forrest Mfg. Co.*

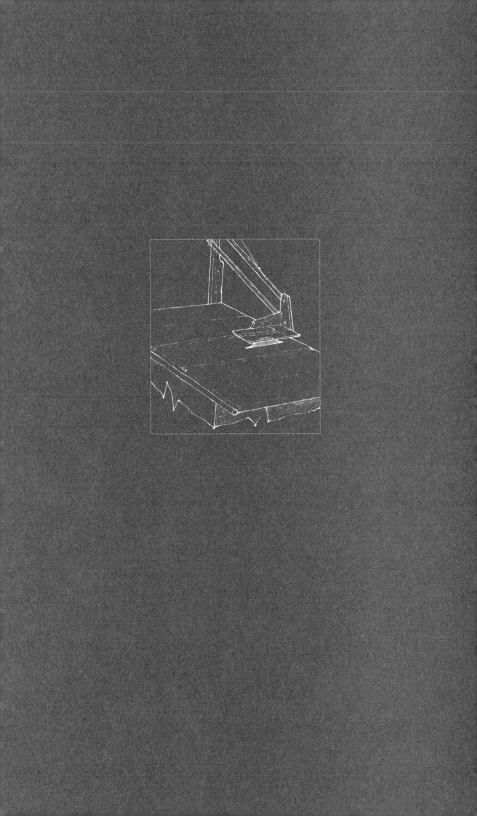

[*Chapter 2*]

SAFETY

Space-Age Saw Guard

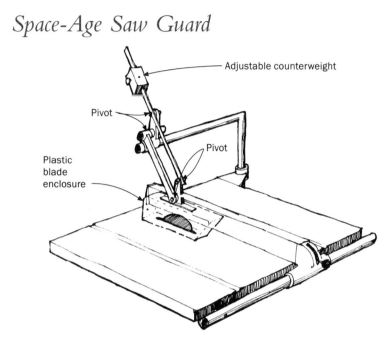

Adjustable counterweight

Pivot

Pivot

Plastic blade enclosure

T HIS TABLESAW GUARD, developed for cutting space-shuttle insulation, holds several advantages over conventional guards. Because it is counterbalanced, the guard makes lighter contact and is easier to operate, especially with thick materials. By sliding the counterweight up or down the arm, the operator can adjust the downward force of the clear-plastic enclosure. The guard doesn't preclude dadoing and grooving operations, which are impossible with some other types of guards. The design was developed by Benjamin R. Dunn and Paul P. Zebus of Rockwell International.

—NASA TECH BRIEFS, *Johnson Space Center, Tex.*

Shopmade Lexan Tablesaw Guard

D URING AN EVENING'S DISCUSSION with several other mechanics, I found that each of us came up with a good reason or two for not using the guards that came with our tablesaws. My long-tested shopmade guard, however, seemed just the sort of thing people would actually use. While it won't control kickback, and won't protect against outright carelessness, it is a real help in my shop.

The guard is a piece of Lexan plastic suspended on a parallelogram-shaped arm fixture that keeps the guard parallel to the table at any height. The guard can be lifted for upright work and blade changes, then quickly lowered for ripping and crosscutting. It keeps knots out of your face and sawdust from cascading behind your safety glasses. The plastic, if cleaned once a day, allows full view of the work without distortion, and its width keeps fingers well away from the blade. The support post should be set back far enough to clear normal crosscut widths, and the entire post should be easily removable for cutting long work.

—ROD GOETTELMANN, *Vincentown, N.J.*

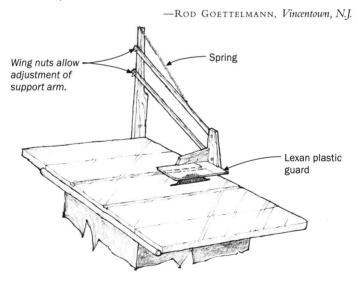

Wing nuts allow adjustment of support arm.

Spring

Lexan plastic guard

Acrylic Tablesaw Guard

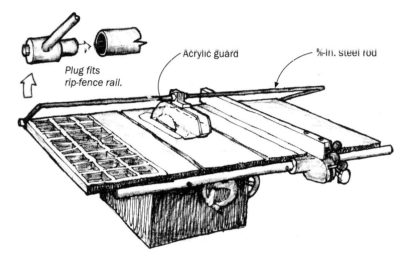

Plug fits rip-fence rail.

Acrylic guard

⅜-in. steel rod

U NLIKE MOST OTHER TABLESAW–BLADE guards, which after a couple of frustrating experiences are left hanging on the wall, this guard is quite usable. The guard's main advantage is that it remains in place for most operations, including dado and molding cuts. If it's not needed for an operation, the guard swings out of the way in seconds, or can easily be removed completely. The inexpensive guard also acts as a hold-down—a safety bonus.

Make the guard shield from ¼-in.-thick clear acrylic. The guard frame is a length of ⅜-in. cold-rolled steel bent into a U shape. Turn two metal or wooden plugs, and attach them to the arms of the frame as shown in the drawing. The plugs should be sized to pivot easily in the holes in the ends of the back rip-fence rail. The frame fits on the saw by springing slightly so that the plugs snap into the holes.

K. L. STEUART, *Ladysmith, B.C., Canada*

Splitter for a Tablesaw

A SPLITTER OR RIVING KNIFE IS a tablesaw fixture that fits behind the blade to keep the saw kerf from closing on the blade as a board is ripped. Depending on the species, the thickness of the wood and how it was dried, there can be a strong tendency for a board to close back on itself, pinching the blade before the ripcut is completed. The splitter keeps the kerf open on the outfeed side of the cut, virtually eliminating kickbacks from pinching. And it's generally safer than jamming a screwdriver in the kerf, as some workers do. Most new saws come with a splitter as standard equipment. If you don't have one, check with the manufacturer. You could also make a knife out of sheet metal or plywood that's slightly thinner than the sawblade you're using and adapt it to your machine.

—RICHARD PREISS, *Charlotte, N.C.,*
from a question by Sol Malkoff, Maitland, Fla.

Blade Changing Made Safer

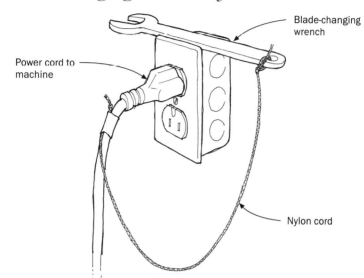

Blade-changing wrench

Power cord to machine

Nylon cord

THIS SIMPLE ARRANGEMENT ENSURES that I never forget to unplug my machines before changing blades or cutters. I've tethered each blade-changing wrench to the power cord for that machine, close to the plug. This means that to change my sawblade, for instance, I must pull the plug and take the wrench and the plug to the saw. For the tether, I use a length of thin nylon cord about 18 in. long. I knot one end of the cord through a hole in the wrench and tape the other end to the cord.

Because I have surface-mounted electrical outlets, I can set the wrench on top of the outlet. With flush outlets, you could use a small nail or screw to hang the wrench so its weight is not on the cord.

You'll get a few very desirable bonuses from this idea: You won't have the disaster of switching on the machine with the blade-changing wrench still engaged, and you'll never misplace the wrench.

—B. BUTTERS, *Doncaster, South Yorkshire, England*

Safely Removing Small Cutoffs

A GOOD WAY TO REMOVE SMALL cutoffs (such as chunks sliced off a dowel) from your tablesaw or bandsaw is to suck them in with your shop vacuum. Fit the vacuum's nozzle through a 2x4 notched to fit its hose diameter. Clamp this setup on the tabletop with the nozzle mounted as close to the cut-off point as possible. When you're done, the parts are neatly collected in the vacuum's barrel.

—DAVID SHAFFER, *Grand Rapids, Mich.*

Place nozzle so it sucks
up small cutoffs.

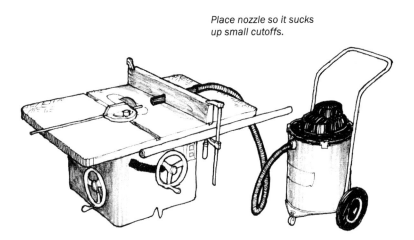

Proper Tablesaw Blade Height

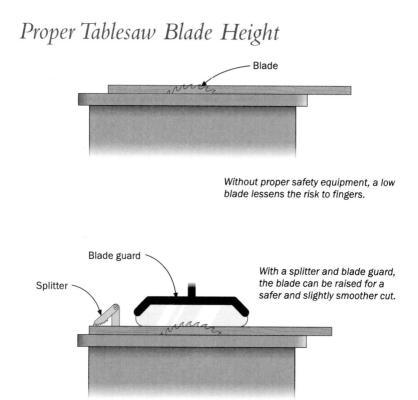

Blade

Without proper safety equipment, a low blade lessens the risk to fingers.

Blade guard

Splitter

With a splitter and blade guard, the blade can be raised for a safer and slightly smoother cut.

HERE IS A LOT of confusion about the proper height to set a tablesaw blade for cutting. For example, one source recommended that the blade never be more than ⅛-in. above the board being cut. Unfortunately, blade height can't ensure that a board will stay on the bed of a tablesaw. Kickback occurs when the teeth on the back of the blade lift the stock off the table and propel it toward the user. Regardless of blade height, the wood tends to rotate away from the fence and into the back of the blade. With the blade spinning at more than 100 mph, there's big trouble when it lifts the board.

There is slightly less chance of kickback when the blade is raised higher through the board. With a high blade, more of the blade's plate surface (the area that does not have teeth) keeps the stock from pivoting as easily as it can when the blade is lower. A high blade will also make cuts that are cleaner, cooler and less likely to burn—especially when using a high-quality, smooth-cutting blade. But the back of the blade tends to pull the stock up off the table, putting you at constant risk. A high blade won't eliminate kickback, and it also introduces a great many other hazards. Simply put, with more of the blade exposed, there is a greater threat of cutting yourself. When I use a splitter and a guard (almost always), I raise the blade so that the gullets clear the board. But without proper safety equipment, using a low blade height is certainly the safest way. For me, lessening the chances of kickback is not a viable option. It's kind of like asking how far through the windshield you'll go if you don't wear a seatbelt. All of the knowledge in the world does little good unless you can physically stop kickback, and using a splitter is the surest way. Until U.S. manufacturers provide more accommodating safety equipment, all woodworkers are at risk.

In short, kickback is a risk no matter how high the blade is raised. Keep the blade low, and use a splitter and blade guard. It's the safest option.

—KELLY MEHLER, *from a question by Ric Bejcek, Phillips, Wisc.*

Tape Tricks for Little Sticks

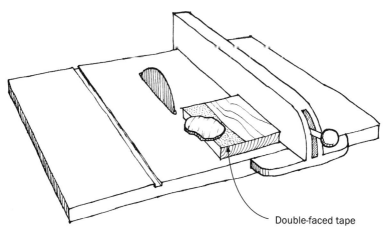

Double-faced tape

I FIND MYSELF MAKING LOTS of little things—small boxes, wooden jewelry and the like. Until I discovered a couple of tricks using double-faced tape, I had a devil of a time sawing the little hunks of wood needed for this kind of work.

To make a straight cut on an odd-shaped, thin slice of wood, run a scrap board through the saw using the rip fence. Stick down a length of double-faced tape to the top of the scrap, peel off the protective paper and mount the odd-shaped slice on the tape for cutting. Don't rely totally on the tape's holding power—hold the piece down with a finger or stick while cutting.

Double-faced tape can also be used effectively in cutting thin strips from the edge of a board. Cut a scrap board with a built-in stop as shown, and mount the tape along the inside edge. The tape holds the slice away from the blade after it is cut. Use the same care in making the cut as if the tape were not there.

—H. N. CAPEN, *Granada Hills, Calif.*

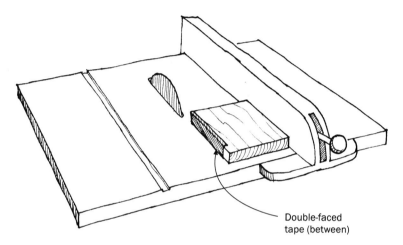

Double-faced
tape (between)

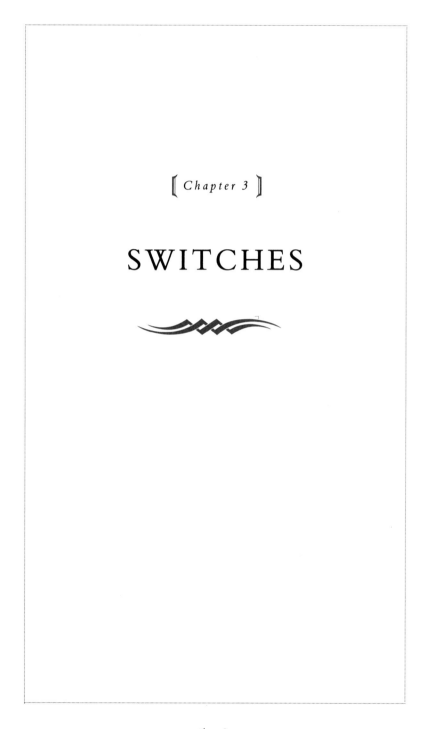

[*Chapter 3*]

SWITCHES

Accessible Saw Switch

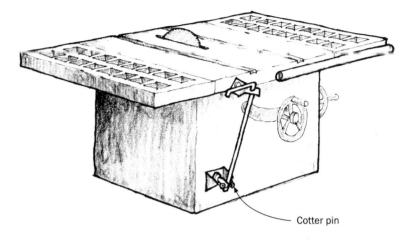

Cotter pin

I RECENTLY BOUGHT A NEARLY new tablesaw, and soon decided that I could not get used to the location of the motor-starting switch, which seemed too far away for comfort and safety. To correct the problem, I attached an extension rod to the switch so that I could shut the saw off instantly without contortions. The rod is supported by an aluminum plate that I twisted in a vise to the correct angle and attached to the saw table in an existing bolt hole.

—ALFRED GORSKI, *Stratford, Conn.*

Replacing a Faulty Switch

I've HEARD SOME COMPLAINTS about the faulty switches that are
installed on some Taiwanese tablesaws, jointers and the like. If your
tool has a faulty switch, one option is simply to replace it with a high-
quality domestic switch. Unfortunately, I'm not aware of any domestic
switch manufacturers making high-quality switches that will directly
interchange with those used on Taiwanese woodworking machines. I
think the best approach would be to complain to the importer, and
try to get a no-charge replacement. If the importer balks, see how
much a replacement switch would cost. I think most of the problems
stem from quality control on the switches, and a new switch that
works out of the box probably will last as long as the machine. This
would be the easiest way to go.

Many offshore manufacturers are very concerned about the per-
ceived quality of their tools and might be willing to provide a replacement at no charge just to make a customer feel more at ease with the
product. However, if you do want to change and upgrade simultaneously and don't mind a bit of fabrication work, then you could use
a domestic, manual motor switch like those made by Cutler Hammer
(Eaton Corp., 4201 N. 27th St., Milwaukee, WI 53216; 414-449-6000).
It would be necessary to route the power cord and motor wiring to
the switch. There's also a possibility on larger machines of using a
magnetic starter. This would give a little extra safety protection to
the machine.

—ED COWERN, *Wallingford, Conn.,*
from a question by Frank Rice, Kingsford, Mich.

Easy-to-Reach Unisaw Switch

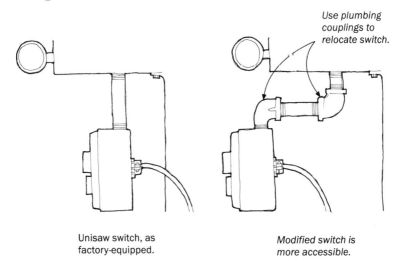

Use plumbing couplings to relocate switch.

Unisaw switch, as factory-equipped.

Modified switch is more accessible.

HERE IS A SIMPLE modification I made to my Delta Unisaw that provides much better access to the on/off switch. The factory-delivered Unisaw has its switch suspended below the table on a ⅜-in. by 4-in. pipe nipple. One end of the nipple screws into the bottom of the saw's cast-iron table, the other into the switch housing. To start or stop the saw, you must grope under the table and back about 8 in. from the edge.

By adding several elbows and a 1-in. nipple, I brought the switch near the front of the saw where it's plainly visible and accessible. The wire doesn't go through the pipe, so there's no wiring change.

—RON KENT, *Kailua, Hawaii*

Foot Switch for Tablesaw

THIS FOOT SWITCH IS for those of us who, with both hands critically occupied on top of the saw table, have wished for a third hand to reach under the table and turn off the saw. I added the switch to my saw primarily for safety reasons but now find its convenience indispensable. The foot switch is simply a hinged paddle that hangs down over the saw's push-button switchbox. I can turn off the saw by bumping the paddle with knee or foot—a short dowel located at just the right spot pushes the off button. A hole through the top part allows normal finger access to the on button and, in fact, offers some protection against the button being pushed accidentally.

—ERIC ESCHEN, *Chico, Calif.*

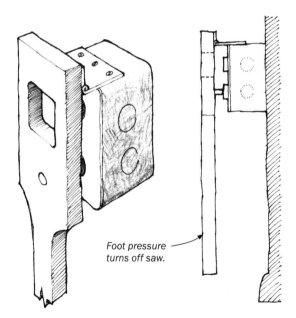

Foot pressure
turns off saw.

Auxiliary Switch for Power Tools

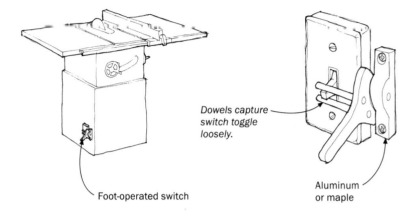

Dowels capture
switch toggle
loosely.

Foot-operated switch

Aluminum
or maple

A FTER EXPERIMENTING WITH A dozen or so locations and types of tablesaw power switches, this is the one I find most convenient and safest to use. I mounted a standard 20-amp light switch low to the left side of the saw as I face the blade. I added an auxiliary, foot-operated lever to the basic switch, so my hands are free to handle the stock. The fingers of the auxiliary-switch lever only loosely trap the actual switch lever in both the on and off position, preventing any damage. I fabricated my latest edition of the switch lever from aluminum, but the original one I made from maple served me long and well.

—DARIO BRISIGHELLA, *Oak Creek, Wisc.*

Auxiliary Tablesaw Switch

H ERE'S HOW I SOLVED the problem of operating the start/stop switch on my tablesaw when ripping large sheets of plywood. I installed a switch identical to the one on the saw at a convenient over-head location near the front of the saw. I wired this switch in series with the saw's switch so that both have to be on to let the saw run, but either switch will turn the saw off.

In use, I first make sure the overhead switch is off, and then I switch on the saw. I get the plywood into position and then reach up and flip on the auxiliary switch. For normal operations, I leave the overhead switch in the on position and use the saw's switch.

—CHARLES W. LEFFERT, *Springfield, N.J.*

Overhead switch
wired in series with
switch on saw.

Refitting a Tablesaw with a Magnetic Switch

ONE BIG DRAWBACK TO THE STANDARD nonmagnetic switches that many tablesaw manufacturers put on their saws is that when there is a power interruption the saw will turn on unexpectedly and sometimes dangerously when the power is restored. The automatic restarting of a machine after a power interruption is a constant problem, and OSHA (Occupational Safety and Health Administration) doesn't allow it in the workplace. Magnetic starters are one solution. On these devices, the start/stop button controls the power to an electromagnetic relay, which does the actual work of connecting the power and motor (line and load) terminals. When the power is interrupted, the electromagnet is deactivated and the power contacts disconnect. When power is restored, the start button must be pressed again to energize the electromagnet so the contact will reconnect and the motor will start. Another advantage of a magnetic starter is it usually includes an in-line overload motor protection circuit. This system uses thermal units (heaters) that one buys extra to suit the motor's amp load.

Magnetic starters range from $150 to $250 and are available from electrical-supply houses. Don't expect the installation to be as simple as a household light switch, though. There are too many variables in starter components. Usually, the actual starter is in a box mounted in an unobtrusive and safe place on the machine, with a small light-switch-size box conveniently mounted elsewhere that encloses the on/off button controls.

If all you want is protection from restart after a power interruption, you can use a product called a Saf-Start-Plug. Delta (800-223-7278) sells them as stock no. 49-350 (other electrical and industrial suppliers also sell them). At about half the cost of a good magnetic starter, these gadgets replace your existing power line and plug with a power line that has a small yellow box with a black button. Any time power is interrupted the button must be pushed to reset the circuit. However, you still have to remember to turn off the machine's switch before resetting the circuit.

If you are uncertain how to install a magnetic starter or Saf-Start-Plug, consult a licensed electrician to be sure it is compatible with the amperage requirements of your motor and that it complies with local codes.

—ROBERT VAUGHAN, *Roanoke, Va.,*
from a question by Gabriel Pons, El Paso, Tex.

Source for an Inexpensive Magnetic Starter?

INSTALLING A MAGNETIC SWITCH on your tablesaw is a desirable upgrade. Unfortunately, when many woodworkers start pricing magnetic switches they get sticker shock. For example, Delta sells a low-voltage magnetic control for the Unisaw that costs about $375. I understand the frustration of trying to find a reasonably priced magnetic starter. After years of looking (and years of installing retrofits for cheap starters gone bad), I've pretty much come to the conclusion that a good-quality magnetic starter is worth the asking price. Delta's low-voltage unit is one of my favorites, and I use it whenever I can because it's so durable and trouble free. In terms of value, it's as good a buy as any other.

—ROBERT VAUGHAN, *Roanoke, Va.,*
from a question by Paul Glasser, Sherwood, Ore.

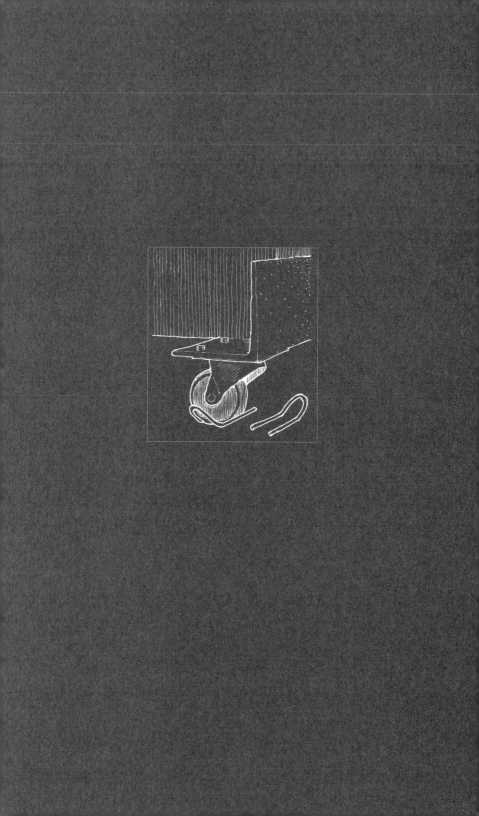

Chapter 4

MOBILE BASES, DOLLIES & MOVERS

Hinged Parking Brake for the Tablesaw

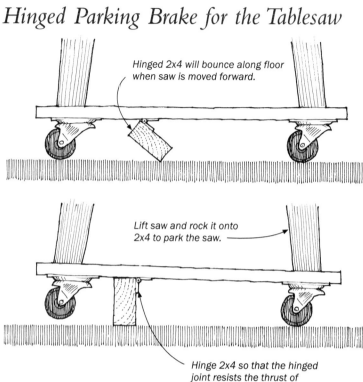

Hinged 2x4 will bounce along floor when saw is moved forward.

Lift saw and rock it onto 2x4 to park the saw.

Hinge 2x4 so that the hinged joint resists the thrust of feeding material.

T O MAKE AN EFFECTIVE parking brake for a tablesaw on casters, simply hinge a 2x4 to a plywood platform under the saw. When you move the saw toward you, the 2x4 will bounce along the floor. When you are ready to use the saw, simply lift the front end slightly and rock the saw backward up onto the 2x4. The hinge joint jams to resist the thrust when feeding material from the front of the saw. A concrete floor will provide enough friction to lock the 2x4; on a wooden floor, you may want to add a rubber strip to the bottom of the 2x4.

—PETE RUSSELL, *Hilton Head Island, S.C.*

Wire Locks Prevent Rolling

TO STOP MY TABLESAW on casters from rolling, I bend 9-in. lengths of ⅛-in.-diameter wire around a ¾-in. pipe. I then bend the curved end of the wire up at about 20°. I slide one of these U-shaped stops under each caster to lock the wheels when the tool is in use. The 20° bend makes them easy to pull out.

— DON GREENFIELD, *Crofton, Ky.*

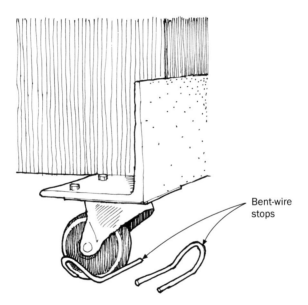

Bent-wire
stops

Wedges Stop Casters from Rolling

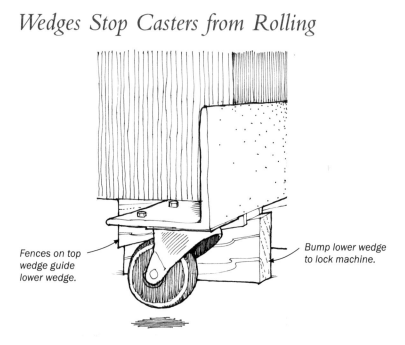

Fences on top wedge guide lower wedge.

Bump lower wedge to lock machine.

I USE LOW-TECH WEDGES to stop my tablesaw from rolling. The lower wedge fits a fenced wedge on the bottom of the saw. A little bump with my foot raises the saw slightly and locks the wedge in place.

—KEITH HACKER, *Scandia, Minn.*

Making Your Tablesaw Portable

I ATTACHED TWO LAWNMOWER WHEELS to the back of my tablesaw to make it portable. In use the tool sits solidly on the floor but can be moved easily by lifting its front end. The wheels rotate on a ½-in. steel axle, and the metal brackets that hold the axle are bolted to the saw's base. I recommend the wheels be mounted no more than ⅛ in. above the floor when the machine is standing upright. This method works well on a tablesaw but I wouldn't advise using it on a top-heavy tool like a bandsaw.

If your machine is heavy, I'd also recommend adding handles to lift the machine. I made mine from oak. The handles normally hang down out of the way; when you want to move the machine, the handles pivot up to the horizontal position where they bump into another bolt that prevents further rotation and provides the leverage to lift the machine. The handles should be placed at a height that gives the most leverage and makes it easy to move the machine around like a wheelbarrow.

—DEAN STEVICK, *Herndon, Va.;*
Peter M. D. Darbishire, Hensall, Ont., Canada; and J. Rufford Harrison

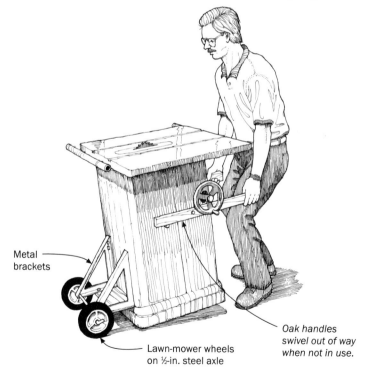

Metal brackets

Lawn-mower wheels on ½-in. steel axle

Oak handles swivel out of way when not in use.

Moving a Tablesaw with Hinged Dollies

Method 1

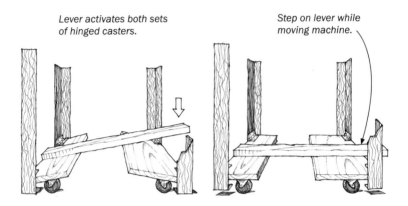

Lever activates both sets of hinged casters.

Step on lever while moving machine.

HINGED DOLLIES HAVE BEEN used for years to move theatrical scenery and props on and off stage in a hurry. Borrowing a stage method, I mounted two heavy-duty casters on each of two pieces of plywood, which are then hinged to the machine's base or legs. A long arm is securely bolted to one of the plywood dollies so that it extends to the front of the machine and serves as a foot pedal. When you step on the pedal, you cause both sets of wheels to push down and to raise the machine an inch or two off the floor.

—BRIAN GANTER, *Foxborough, Mass.*

I USE A TWO-WHEEL DOLLY with a simple spring latch to hold the wheels in the down position. The dolly is hinged to two legs of the saw and has a foot pedal bolted to it. The foot pedal not only raises the saw onto the dolly but also serves as a latch. A 1x2 extends down from a crosspiece attached to the other two legs of the machine's base. When the lever clears the 1x2, it springs back and prevents the lever from moving back up. To lower the tool stand back to the floor, I disengage the latch with a little sideways kick that leaves my foot in position to control the upward motion of the lever and prevent the tool from dropping heavily.

—DAVID ROGERS, *Thornhill, Ont., Canada*

Method 2

Step on lever to activate hinged casters and lock latch.

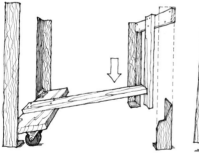 

Latch holds lever while machine is moved.

Folding Saw-Dolly

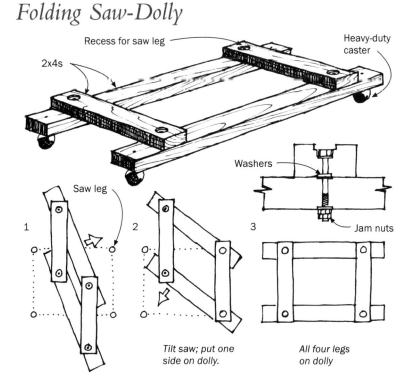

Recess for saw leg

Heavy-duty caster

2x4s

Washers

Saw leg

1

2

3

Jam nuts

Tilt saw; put one
side on dolly.

All four legs
on dolly

I HAVE TO SHARE MY SHOP SPACE WITH an automobile and other
"foreign objects," so from time to time I have to move my tablesaw,
which is on a four-legged, sheet-metal stand. To avoid having to drag
the saw across the floor, I made a dolly that collapses like a panto-
graph. The folding action allows me to load the saw on the dolly one
side at a time as shown in the sequence above.

—ROBERT E. WARREN, *Camarillo, Calif.*

Flip-Down Wheels

T HIS SIMPLE FLIP-DOWN AXLE fits tool stands with bent sheet-metal
legs. First, slide two wheels on a ⅜-in. steel rod, adding washers
and cotter pins to keep the wheels in position. Bend the rod to a wide
U-shape, as shown, and install the axle through holes drilled in two
legs. The holes should be located so that when you lift up the end of
the stand and flip down the axle with your foot the axle will bear
against the inside bend of the leg, effectively locking itself in position.

—JEFF LORMANS, *Dunedin, New Zealand*

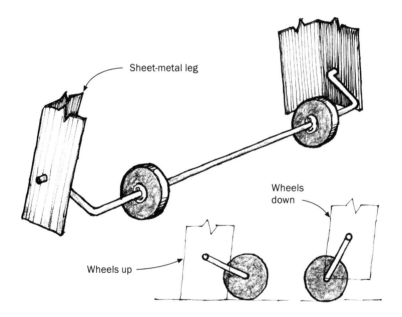

Sheet-metal leg

Wheels
down

Wheels up

Mobile Tool Base

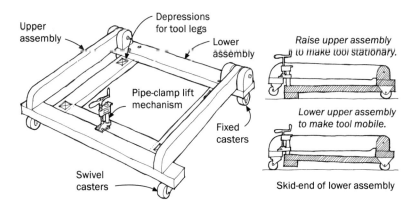

If, like me, you have collected more large stationary tools than you have room to store, this mobile base will enable you to move heavy equipment around your shop.

The base consists of an upper and a lower assembly. The lower assembly has fixed casters at the rear and a wood skid at the front. Tool legs sit in depressions cut in the lower assembly. As long as the skid is on the floor, the weight of the tool keeps the assembly from moving. When the skid is lifted from the floor by the pipe-clamp lifting mechanism, weight is shifted to swivel casters on the upper assembly, and the base is free to roll.

Construction of the wooden parts is simple. All pieces are cut from standard 2x4s, except the back part of the lower assembly, which is ripped from a 2x6. For the lifting mechanism, use the screw end of a Pony No. 50 pipe clamp with a 7½-in. length of ¾-in. pipe. Drill two holes through the face of the clamp, and install wood screws to hold it to the upper assembly. Drill a hole into the skid for the pipe, and position it in the lower assembly so that the wheels on the upper assembly just touch the ground when the clamp screw is at its midpoint of travel. Drill a ⁵⁄₁₆ in. hole through the pipe, and pin it into the lower assembly with a ¼-in. lag screw. Tightening the clamp raises the skid end of the lower assembly, allowing the mobile base to roll.

—JEFFREY D. ANDERSON, *Melbourne, Fla.*

Lawn-Mower Height Adjusters on Tool Stands

B Y ATTACHING LAWN-MOWER wheel-height adjusters to your tool stands, you can add portability without disfiguring the equipment. In my case, I fitted the height adjusters (Arnold model HA700) along with 6-in. lawn-mower wheels to the two front legs of my 140-lb. scroll-saw stand. The adjusters and wheels are readily available at small-engine repair shops and are simple to attach by following the manufacturer's instructions on the back of the package. Just be sure that the stand will sit on the floor when the wheels are all the way up.

—DONALD G. HULSEY, *Tucson, Ariz.*

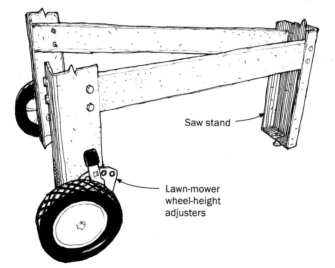

Saw stand

Lawn-mower wheel-height adjusters

Heavy-Machine Shuffler

Step down on raised end to
move heavy machine.

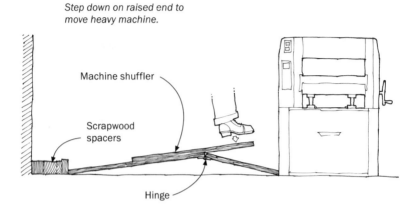

Machine shuffler

Scrapwood
spacers

Hinge

THIS "SHUFFLER" IS A SIMPLE DEVICE I use to move heavy
woodworking machines around my workshop. With it I can
shift the base of the machine 4 in. or 5 in. without rollers, wedges or
back pains.

The device is made from three pieces of 1x4 scraps, joined and
hinged as shown in the sketch. To use it, I place scrap-wood spacers
between the end of the shuffler and a convenient wall or post so that
the center of the shuffler is a few inches off the floor. Then I press
down on the raised end with my foot, moving the machine about
an inch or so. I repeat the process, adding more spacers until the
machine is where I want it. The only drawback is that if you use too
many spacers, they tend to spring out. So if you've got to shift the
machine more than about 6 in., just rebuild the shuffler with a longer
piece of scrap.

—CHRIS YONGE, *Englewood, N.J.*

Knockdown Saw Stand

B ECAUSE I DON'T HAVE enough space in my tiny shop for a
tablesaw, I designed this lightweight, knockdown tablesaw stand
that stores away in three flat pieces. When I need my tablesaw, I simply
set up the stand outside the door of my shop and mount the saw.
There are no screws, pins or pegs, so the stand can be put together
in seconds.

To make the stand in about an hour, all you'll need is an 8-ft.-long
1x10 and a handful of 1¼-in. plaster wallboard screws. Then follow the
construction details shown in the sketch. The stand requires a snug fit
of the leg assemblies into the cleats, so pay special attention when you
attach the cleats to the underside of the top.

—RAY MAYOTTE, *Worcester, Mass.*

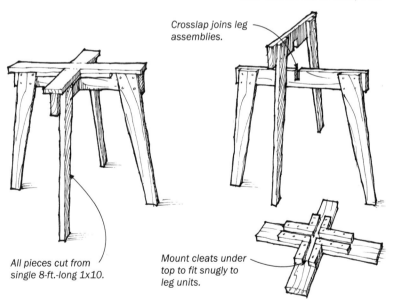

Crosslap joins leg
assemblies.

All pieces cut from
single 8-ft.-long 1x10.

Mount cleats under
top to fit snugly to
leg units.

OUTFEED TABLES
&
ROLLER SUPPORTS

Roller Support for Ripping

Rolling pin

H ERE'S AN INEXPENSIVE, ADJUSTABLE roller support for long stock as it leaves the tablesaw or jointer. The support is made from an old rolling pin and a sturdy frame. The handgrips of the rolling pin are each supported by notched blocks, which are adjustable for height by means of a bolt and wing nut.

—ROGIER DE WEEVER, *Kelowna, B.C., Canada*

Refinements on the Roller Support

T HE HEART OF MY ROLLER HORSE for supporting long stock off the tablesaw, radial-arm saw or jointer is a worn-out typewriter platen. These are available, often just for the asking, from typewriter service shops, and they stay truer than wooden rollers, an advantage particularly for jointer-feed support. The wedges between the roller carriage and the horse allow for fine height adjustment.

—D. KERMAN, *Swampscott, Mass.*

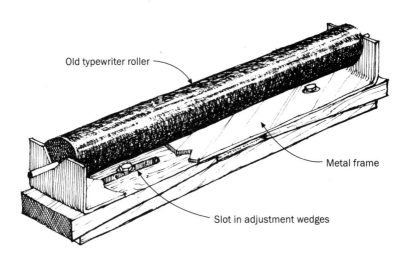

Old typewriter roller

Metal frame

Slot in adjustment wedges

Roller-Stand Adjustment Mechanism

Tightening bolt fits T-nut pressed into back side of cover plate.

T HE MAIN DIFFERENCES BETWEEN this roller stand and other designs I've seen are the ease of adjustment and the tilting head. The tilting head, together with the three-legged base, makes it easy to cope with a shop floor that, like mine, isn't level.

The arrangement for adjusting the height consists of a bolt threaded through a T-nut pressed into the inside of a cover plate, as shown in the drawing. The head of the bolt is captured in an oak knob, which permits easy hand tightening. The bolt does not bear directly on the sliding dowel but on a loose wooden insert set in the post. This permits smoother adjustments and prevents the bolt from chewing up the dowel. The insert itself is protected by a brass wear strip.

—TIMOTHY D. ANDERSON, *St. Paul, Minn.*

Ball-Bearing Furniture Casters
for Outfeed Support

THE KEY TO AN EFFICIENT TABLESAW ripping support or panel-crosscut support is a smooth-working, friction-free roller. I've found nothing that fills this requirement better or cheaper than ball-bearing furniture casters.

Fasten several of the casters in a close-spaced pattern on top of a homemade, adjustable stand. Or, for instant support, fasten eight or ten casters to the end of a 2-ft.-long 2x12. Then clamp the 2x12 in a Workmate vise at the right height. The casters roll easily in any direction, so you can put the support just where it's needed. There's no need to fuss with the orientation of the support as there is with other types.

—LARRY JOSEPH, *Alva, Okla.*

Grid Expands Saw Table

Be sure when spacing crosspieces to keep joints away from mounting holes.

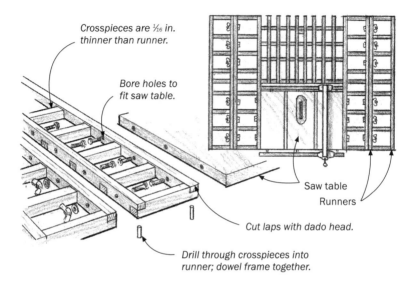

Crosspieces are ⅟₁₆ in. thinner than runner.

Bore holes to fit saw table.

Saw table

Runners

Cut laps with dado head.

Drill through crosspieces into runner; dowel frame together.

H ERE'S HOW I EXPANDED the size of the top of my tablesaw. Most tablesaws have bolt holes in the sides of the table for adding extensions. I used these bolt holes to add extensions cut from 1-in.-thick, well-dried maple. The width of each piece should match the thickness of the apron on your saw table. To ensure that all the pieces would be identical, I ripped all the components at the same saw setting, first cutting the runners that extend from front to back, then cutting the crosspieces. The crosspieces should be about ⅟₁₆ in. thinner than the runners so the stock won't catch as you run it across the table. Don't make the extensions too wide; I like 12-in.-wide units.

Because of the way the holes are bored, you can always bolt narrower units together to expand the table, if necessary. You might add a leg to support larger extensions.

After cutting the runners, clamp them to the table and mark the locations of the holes so they can be drilled accurately. Turn the rails around and drill the same holes on the other ends. This double set of holes enables you to attach either end of the extension to the saw. It also lets you clamp the side grids to the middle grid bolted to the back of the saw, which adds to the rigidity of the extensions. After boring the holes, use a dado head to cut the lap joints for joining the runners to the crosspieces, being careful to keep the joints away from the bolt holes. To assemble the extension, I first built the frame of each grid by drilling all the way through the end-of-frame crosspiece and into the ends of the runners, so I could dowel and glue the pieces together. Make sure you keep everything flat and square. The remaining crosspieces can be glued and screwed or tacked in place after the frame is glued together. When I'm working with a large piece and need to mount a fence on the grid, I use a Clamp 'N Tool guide manufactured by Tru-Grip Clamps (Griset Industries, P.O. Box 10114, Santa Ana, CA 92771).

—HANS SPORBECK, *Pewaukee, Wisc.,*
from a question by R.L. Marcotte, Penfield, N.Y.

Roller Support for Crosscutting

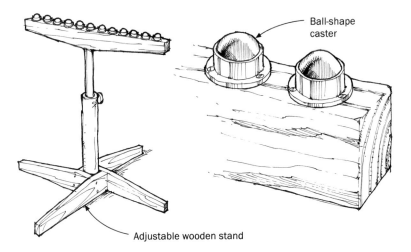

Ball-shape caster

Adjustable wooden stand

ALTHOUGH THERE ARE MANY freestanding roller stands available for supporting work being ripped on the tablesaw, I've never seen a similar support for crosscutting. The support I developed has served me well in both ripping and crosscutting. Its principal component is a unique ball-shape caster (available from Rockler Woodworking and Hardware (4365 Willow Dr., Medina, MN 55340; 800-279-4441; www.rockler.com). The caster rides on ball bearings, allowing smooth movement. Keep them clean and free from sawdust or they'll clog and won't run freely. The wooden stand is adjustable and has a weighted base.

—WILLIAM A. LEMKE, *Hendersonville, N.C.*

Folding Infeed Table
Quickly Dismounts from Saw

B ECAUSE I'M OLDER AND work alone, I need all the help I can get when feeding big, clumsy sheets of plywood into my tablesaw. But I just don't have room in my cramped shop for another table. So I designed this folding table, about 2 ft. wide and 4 ft. long, with hinged legs on one end and a ledge on the other end, which hooks over the rip-fence rail. The legs are cut a little overlong, for a slightly upward slant to the table that seems to help hold it in place. When I'm through ripping, I fold up the legs and lean the table against the wall.

—CLIFF NATHAN, *Studio City, Calif.*

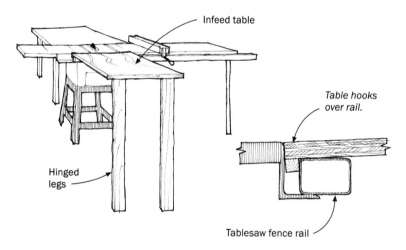

Infeed table

Table hooks
over rail.

Hinged
legs

Tablesaw fence rail

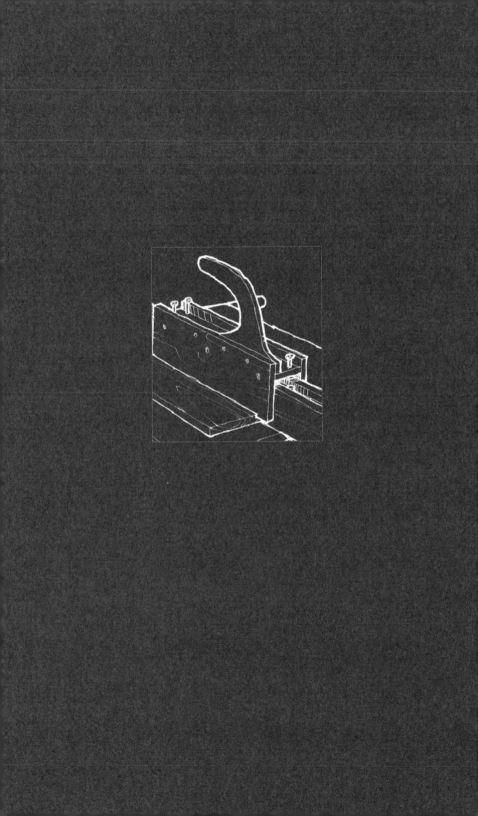

[*Chapter 6*]

PUSH
STICKS

Improved Push Stick

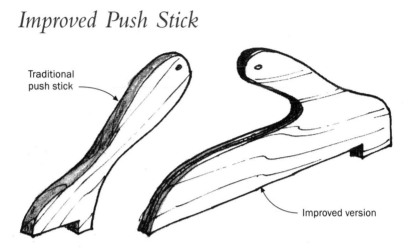

Traditional push stick

Improved version

IN THE PAST 11 YEARS I'VE WORKED in several shops, from a furniture factory to a custom cabinet shop, and taught some high-school woodworking as well. As you might imagine, I've seen my share of tablesaw push sticks, most of which resemble the design shown in the left drawing above. The major shortcoming of this design is that it does little to counteract the tablesaw's tendency to lift the work off the table.

The alternative design, shown on the right, ensures a downward thrust on the work. In production runs, this design is safer and less fatiguing because you need only push forward, rather than forward and down. You can make wide push sticks from solid wood, but for narrow ones choose plywood; otherwise the step on the bottom of the stick may split off.

—ANGELO DALUISIO, *Lancaster, N.Y.*

Handsaw-Handle Push Stick

THE NOTCHED PUSH STICKS used in many shops seemed unsafe and unwieldy to me, so I designed a push stick that lets me concentrate on sawing boards instead of fingers. First, I traced the handle from a comfortable handsaw onto a piece of scrap, 10 in. by 18 in., positioning the handle at an angle that keeps my fingers away from a fully raised blade. I made a notch and ended it well ahead of the heel. This positioning contributes to the push stick's safety: If you carelessly lower your hand, the end of the stick will bottom out on the saw table, pivoting the notch up and releasing its grip on the end of the board. It will still hold the work, but it's a reminder that you're courting trouble.

I've also found that two push sticks are better than one. With a second small notch at the end of both, either can be used to hold stock against the rip fence while you push with the other. I applied nonstick stair tape to the end notch to improve the grip on the work.

—DAVID L. WISELEY, *Waters, Mich.*

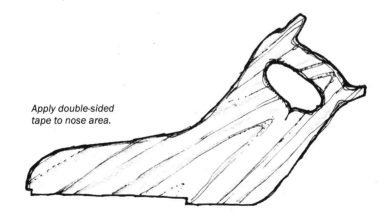

Apply double-sided
tape to nose area.

Holding Push Sticks with Velcro

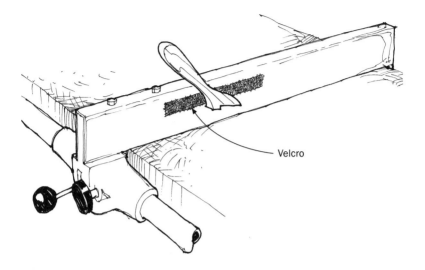

Velcro

FRUSTRATED AT NEVER HAVING my push sticks on my tablesaw when I need them, I glued a strip of hook-and-loop fastener on the right side of my rip fence and the mating fastener material on the sides of my push sticks. The push sticks now stand at attention on the rip fence, ready to be grabbed when needed. Most fastener strips now comes with a peel-off sticky back that should fasten the material well enough. This tip could be used for many accessories and tools around the shop.

—DAVID CRAWFORD, *Brownsboro, Tex.*

En Garde Push Stick

I N THE SHOP WHERE WE MANUFACTURE magic props, a tablesaw kickback caused 43 stitches worth of damage. That's when I decided to design this special push stick. The guard protects the fingers and hands, which are most exposed to potential damage during a kickback.

To make the push stick, I started with a stainless-steel custard bowl about 5 in. or so across, and then I added two turned wooden disks, one inside and one outside the bowl. A mortise through the disks accepts a removable push stick, which locks into place with a dowel pin. Yeah, it looks like overkill—but remember—we only have 10 fingers.

—CARL WILLIAMS, *Pasadena, Calif.*

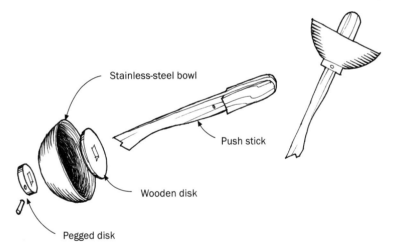

Stainless-steel bowl

Push stick

Wooden disk

Pegged disk

Push Stick for Ripping Narrow Strips

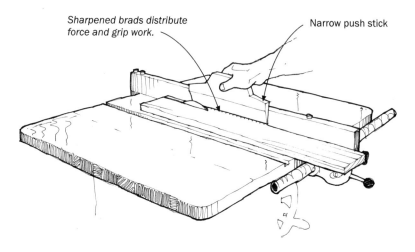

Sharpened brads distribute force and grip work.

Narrow push stick

Ripping narrow strips on a tablesaw felt risky until I improvised a pusher with multiple sharpened brads. With this device, I can push the workpiece forward and, at the same time, press it tightly against the fence to ensure accurate width. The pusher gives me secure control of the wood and also keeps my fingers well away from the saw. Because the force is distributed over multiple points, penetration into the wood is not noticeable. I have been using this device for 40 years, so its 30 minutes of construction time has been a good investment.

—Richard Koontz, *Camp Hill, Pa.*

Push Stick for Rabbeting Thin Pieces

THIS PUSH STICK IS customized for slotting or rabbeting thin pieces, such as picture-frame parts, where the blade does not protrude above the workpiece. The saw kerf in the push stick presses on the outer edge of the work, holding it both down and against the fence. The length of the pusher allows it to bear against the whole length of most workpieces. The stop screwed to the end of the pusher should protrude just enough to hook over the end of the work and push it along.

—ABIJAH REED, *Newton Center, Mass.*

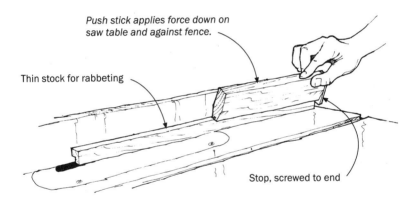

Push stick applies force down on saw table and against fence.

Thin stock for rabbeting

Stop, screwed to end

Rip-Fence Straddling Push Stick

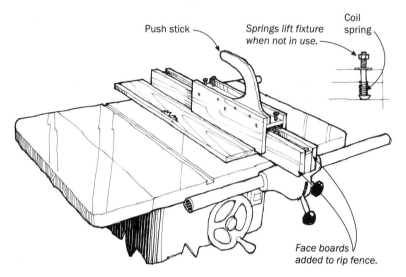

Push stick

Springs lift fixture
when not in use.

Coil
spring

Face boards
added to rip fence.

THIS FENCE-STRADDLING PUSH STICK was originally designed to fit a Biesemeyer fence, but it could be adapted to practically any fence fitted with auxiliary face boards, as shown in the drawing. For added convenience, I installed plungers made from coil springs and bolts to raise the push stick when not in use.

—BILL HATCH, *Greensboro, N.C.*

"L" Push Stick

FIFTEEN YEARS AGO, NORMAN BUCHHOLZ showed me the best push stick that I have ever seen. It works equally well at the jointer and the tablesaw; either arm can be used as a handle. Make the sticks from ¾-in. scrap plywood, and jettison used ones regularly.

—M. FELIX MARTI, *Ridgway, Colo.*

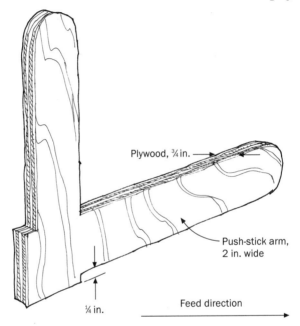

Plywood, ¾ in.

Push-stick arm, 2 in. wide

¼ in.

Feed direction

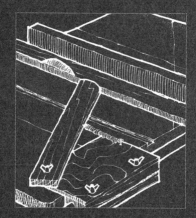

HOLD-INS
&
HOLD-DOWNS

Nonskid Finger-Pressure Boards

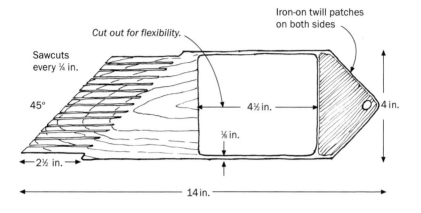

A SMALL BOARD CUT 45° ACROSS the grain and kerfed to form fingers is quite useful for holding work against the fence in shaping and ripping operations. But the fingers jam unless you shim the board off the table, and the board tends to move under the clamps and lose tension. I solved both these problems by applying twill, iron-on patches sold for repairing work clothes.

—R. P. SYKES, *Thousand Oaks, Calif.*

Nonslip Fingerboards

FINGERBOARDS PERFORM MUCH MORE effectively if you screw them to tapped holes in the saw table rather than clamping them. Clamped fingerboards don't lie flat, and they can slip and lose pressure against the work.

To make the fingerboard, saw kerfs ⅛ in. or so apart in the end of an angled 1x3. Rout two ¼-in. slots down the centerline of the fingerboard—one at the head, one at the tail. Now set the fingerboard in position on the saw so it will exert pressure just ahead of the blade, and mark the center of each slot on the saw table with a punch. Drill and tap holes into the table at these points. Lock the unit in place with cap screws or bolts threaded into the tapped holes.

—BEN ERICKSON, *Eutaw, Ala.*

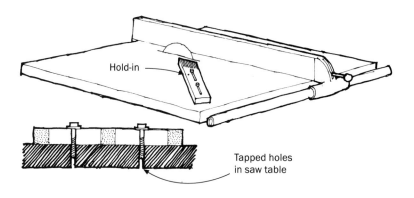

Hold-in

Tapped holes
in saw table

Self-Clamping Featherboard

Rubber-padded
hinge grips table.

M OST WOODWORKERS RECOGNIZE THE value of using a feather-board when feeding narrow stock through a saw or router table. But too often we fail to use the device because it's simply too much trouble to clamp and adjust. This featherboard is no more trouble to adjust and use than a rip fence. It has paid for itself many times over in time and material savings. My version grips the table by means of a rubber-padded hinge, activated by a bolt running through a T-nut, as shown in the sketch; the handwheel is held on by epoxy. You could adapt the design to grip securely on virtually any rip-fence rails.

—BERT WHITCHURCH, *Rockaway Beach, Mo.*

Featherboard Clamps to Fence Rail

I FINALLY GOT TIRED OF the clumsy business of clamping a feather-board to the saw table, and then tediously reclamping it each time to adjust it to the width of a new workpiece. This simple solution took less than an hour to make and works perfectly.

It consists of two parts: a featherboard and a sliding-base assembly. Custom-fit the sliding base to your front fence rail so that it can move anywhere along the front edge of the saw table and be locked in place with wing nuts or wedges. My sliding assembly is made to fit the T-slots of the Delta Unifence arrangement (the one in the drawing is shown on the more usual, round Unisaw rails). The featherboard pivots on a bolt and is kept in tension against the workpiece by a spring.

—ARTHUR KAY, *Tucson, Ariz.*

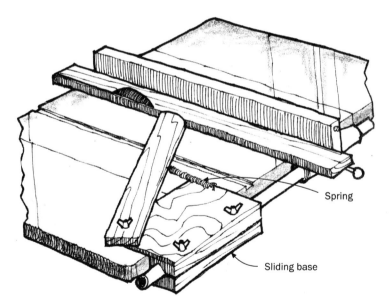

Spring

Sliding base

Featherboard Rides in Miter-Gauge Slot

Strip and block hold featherboard.

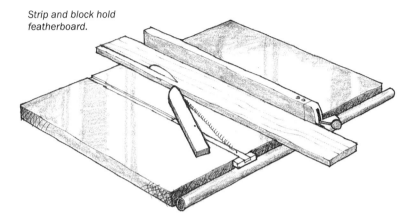

Here is a featherboard that is very quick to install and remove. The hold-in part of the featherboard is fastened to a strip of ½-in.-thick wood, which is a snug fit in the miter-gauge slot. A small block on the end prevents the strip from sliding toward the back of the saw. The featherboard itself is fastened to this strip from below by a screw and is held in tension against the stock being ripped by a spring. I reversed the traditional shape of the end of the featherboard so that it would bear on the stock as closely as possible to the front of the blade, yet still clear the teeth when the stock being ripped passes through.

—Harold W. Books, *North Platte, Neb.*

Featherboard from Scrap Strips

PERIODICALLY, AS I'M PROCESSING lumber on the tablesaw, I'll generate a large number of small flexible off-rips that are identical in size. A few years ago, I started recycling some of these scraps into useful materials—featherboards.

I start with enough 1-ft.-long pieces to make a board 3 in. or 4 in. wide; dab glue on just the first 2 in. or so of each piece, and clamp the lot together. If they misalign slightly during clamp-up, I just run the newly milled "board" through the planer and trim the end to the angle I want. Now, the featherboard is ready for use. I like to screw two featherboards to a baseboard, and then clamp the base to the tablesaw. I set the featherboards so that one contacts the workpiece just before it enters the blade and the other just after it exits.

—M. FELIX MARTI, *Monroe, Ore.*

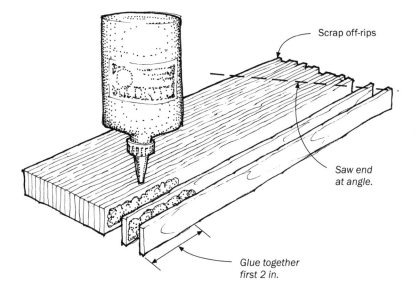

Scrap off-rips

Saw end at angle.

Glue together first 2 in.

Hold-In and Hold-Down in One Device

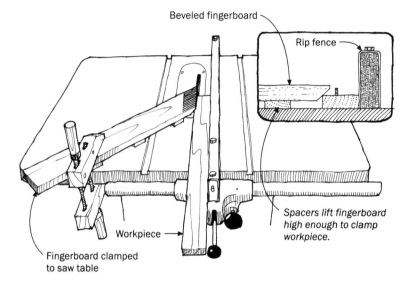

Beveled fingerboard

Rip fence

Spacers lift fingerboard
high enough to clamp
workpiece.

Workpiece

Fingerboard clamped
to saw table

FINGERBOARDS ARE GREAT FOR holding boards against a fence or down on a table, but they usually can't do both jobs very well at the same time. However, if you cut a bevel on the leading edge, as shown above, the fingerboard can accomplish both tasks. Raise the fingerboard off the table with spacers to make it hit the stock at the right place.

—RICHARD CHIROS, *Marlboro, Mass.*

Rail-Clamping Featherboard

I REGULARLY USE A FEATHERBOARD when ripping stock in my shop. However, it is often difficult to clamp a traditional loose featherboard to the table quickly and securely. To eliminate this problem, I made a hard maple saddle that rides on my rectangular fence rail and screwed a featherboard to the top of the saddle at about 45°. I salvaged the locking knob from an old compressor regulator, but similar knobs are available from Rockler Woodworking and Hardware (4365 Willow Dr., Medina, MN 55340; 800-279-4441; www.rockler.com).

To prevent damage to the fence rail, I inset a wooden strip under the knob stud, which is counterbored to accept two loosely fitting screws. I can quickly lock the featherboard assembly in any position along the fence rail and, with a quick twist of the knob, remove the whole assembly to make way for crosscutting. By varying the saddle design, this method could be used with any fence rail, such as the tubular type.

—BERT B. BOYD, *Salem, Va.*

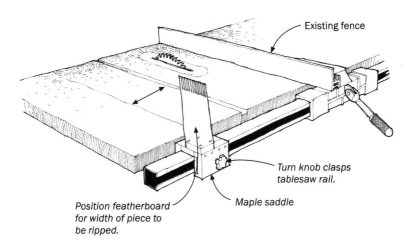

Existing fence

Turn knob clasps
tablesaw rail.

Position featherboard
for width of piece to
be ripped.

Maple saddle

Rubber Tire Hold-In

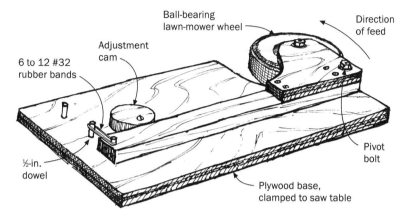

Ball-bearing lawn-mower wheel

Direction of feed

Adjustment cam

6 to 12 #32 rubber bands

½-in. dowel

Pivot bolt

Plywood base, clamped to saw table

THE SIMPLE FIXTURE USING a lawn-mower wheel sketched at right has made featherboard hold-ins obsolete in my shop. I have two: one as shown and the other a mirror image of the first. I use them on both the tablesaw and the router table for ripping, cutting grooves, shaping, and other operations.

The advantages of this fixture over featherboards are significant: Feed friction is greatly reduced, hold-down pressure is adjustable and consistent (even when the stock is uneven) and setup is quicker and easier. Because fore/aft friction is all but eliminated, there is little tendency for the fixture to squirm and turn under the clamp. Only one clamp will keep it in place, even on a waxed saw table. The disadvantage is that there is no kickback resistance as with featherboards. But kickback can be all but eliminated by using sharp, clean blades and carefully setting up for each cut.

The idea for rubber-tire pressure wheels is not mine; similar fixtures are used on large power-feed industrial woodworking machines. I suppose the wheel could be cut from plywood to save the extra few dollars spent on the ball-bearing lawn mower wheel and special axle bolt. But I find it comforting to see the rubber tire flatten a bit as it pushes the work against the rip fence.

—BOB DeFRANCES, *Delray Beach, Fla.*

Leaf-Spring Hold-In

I WOULDN'T USE THIS GADGET for ripping, because it would tend to close the kerf, but it's a solution to the problem of holding the feedstock when using a molding head on the tablesaw or for holding it against the fence on a router table. Start with a 1½-in.-sq. length of hardwood. Cut a V-groove in one side (to fit the pipe of a pipe clamp), and rip a ¼-in. slot in the other side. Screw the hardwood to a pipe clamp long enough to fit your saw table or router table.

Now install several ¼-in. flat steel springs in the groove. These springs, available at hardware stores, are used to repair old double-hung windows with broken weight ropes. Clamp the hold-in across the machine table in a position so that the springs flatten as the work is pushed through. To prevent the work from moving upward, it's a good idea to use this pipe clamp hold-in in conjunction with a fingerboard that will press the work to the table.

—RAYMOND YOHE, *Altoona, Pa.*

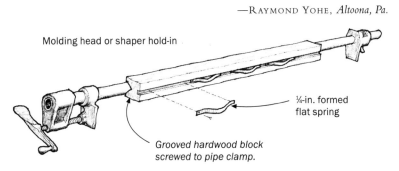

Molding head or shaper hold-in

¼-in. formed
flat spring

Grooved hardwood block
screwed to pipe clamp.

Hold-Ins for Molding Head

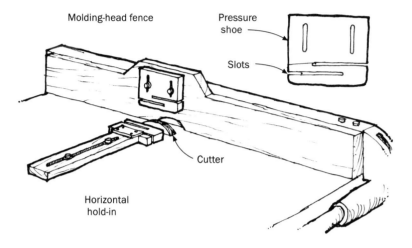

Molding-head fence

Pressure shoe

Slots

Cutter

Horizontal hold-in

THE MOLDING HEAD FOR THE TABLESAW is a valuable tool. But without the proper hold-ins it is practically impossible to shape thin stock without chattering. The hold-in fixtures I use to overcome this handicap consist of an auxiliary fence and a horizontal hold-in. The auxiliary fence is a maple 1x3, which screws to the saw's rip fence. Since this fence may cover part of the rotating cutterhead, it's a good idea to cut a recess into the fence beforehand by raising the cutterhead into the fence. The top of the fence is fitted with an adjustable pressure shoe that holds the work to the saw table.

Make the pressure shoe from a stick of maple by sawing two (or more) saw kerfs from opposite ends. This gives the shoe some spring, allowing it to adjust to minor variations in thickness and to damp out any chattering.

The horizontal hold-in is simply a slotted arm fitted with another pressure shoe. It holds the work firmly against the fence. The arm locks in place with cap screws that fit tapped holes in the table.

Design the fence and hold-in so you can reverse them and use them on either side of the saw's rip fence. This will allow you to take full advantage of both left-hand and right-hand cutter designs.

—WALTER O. MENNING, *LaSalle, Ill.*

Flexible Hold-In

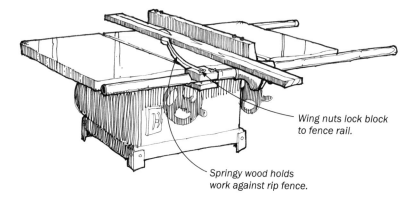

Wing nuts lock block
to fence rail.

Springy wood holds
work against rip fence.

M OST FEATHERBOARDS OR HOLD-INS utilize an angled board
with numerous saw kerfs cut into one end. The flexibility of
these featherboards is pretty limited, so they must invariably be reset
after every cut. The alternative design shown in the drawing offers a
much greater range of flexibility and requires fewer adjustments as ripping progresses. The bandsawn spring is dadoed into a split block that
slides on, and locks to, the rip-fence rail for quick adjustment. The
length of the spring and the strength of its action can be tailored to
suit. Hickory or pecan are common springy woods that adapt well to
this type of use.

—BERT G. WHITCHURCH, *Hemet, Calif.*

Spring-Loaded Hold-Ins

THIS PAIR OF TABLESAW HOLD-INS uses gate-closer springs to apply pressure on the piece being cut. I added an old shaft bearing to the front hold-in to reduce friction. Since my saw has a T-slotted miter-gauge track, I designed the wing-nut-and-aluminum-plate locking device to take advantage of it. On saws that don't have a T-slotted track, just size the hold-ins so they can be press-fit into the miter-gauge track.

—FRANK USHER, *Nepean, Ont., Canada*

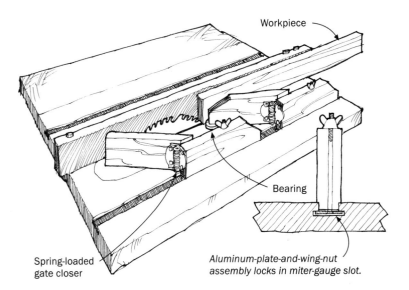

Workpiece

Bearing

Spring-loaded
gate closer

Aluminum-plate-and-wing-nut
assembly locks in miter-gauge slot.

RIP-FENCE
&
MITER-GAUGE
IMPROVEMENTS

Setting a Saw Fence with Calipers

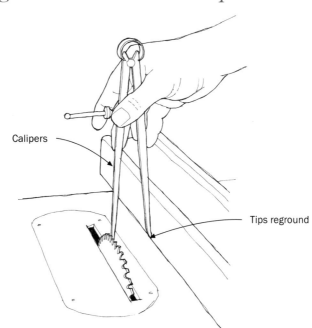

Calipers

Tips reground

I HAVE ALWAYS FOUND IT AWKWARD to set the rip fence of a tablesaw parallel to the blade using a ruler or tape measure, because I have to crane my neck over the saw table to read the measurement at the back of the blade. Also, using both edges of the tape or ruler, which may not have the same unit of measurement, can cause confusion. I now use a large set of inside calipers with a maximum extension of 12 in. for cuts within that range. I have ground the tips of these calipers to give a minimum reading of ¼ in. The calipers are set to the desired width of cut, and by alternately placing them between the fence and the front and rear of the blade, I can not only see any necessary adjustment but also feel it.

—KENT MCDONNELL, *Newcastle, Ont., Canada*

Laminate Closes Gap under the Rip Fence

TO PREVENT THIN STOCK AND PLASTIC LAMINATE from slipping under a rip fence, buy a scrap of magnetic sign material and use spray glue to attach it to a strip of laminate that's the length of your fence. Stick the strip to the face of your rip fence, and slide it down, flush with the tabletop.

—ROD BARNARD, *Seattle, Wash.*

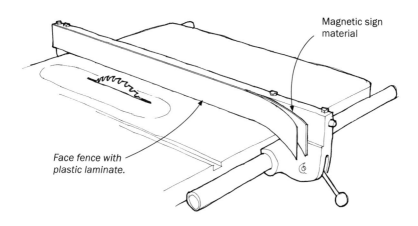

Magnetic sign material

Face fence with plastic laminate.

Quick Fence-Reset Fixture
for the Tablesaw

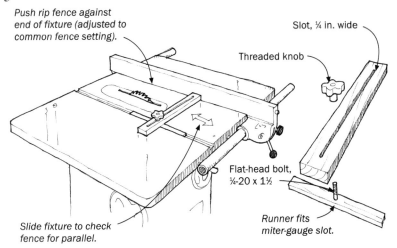

Push rip fence against end of fixture (adjusted to common fence setting).

Slot, ¼ in. wide

Threaded knob

Flat-head bolt, ¼-20 x 1½

Slide fixture to check fence for parallel.

Runner fits miter-gauge slot.

Forty-five years ago, I worked in a large shop where I cut out parts for store cases, 50 or so per tablesaw setup. In some instances, we had to mill orders to slightly different dimensions and then return to the original saw settings. This required tedious machine changeovers, particularly in setting and resetting the fence. I've come up with an idea that would have been valuable to me a half century ago.

This simple fixture consists of two hardwood bars that form an adjustable cross. I sized the bottom bar to fit the tablesaw miter-gauge slot and routed a slot in the top bar. It slides back and forth over a bolt and can be locked in place with a knob. To use the fixture, push it into the miter-gauge slot, move the upper bar against the rip fence and tighten the knob. Check fore and aft on the fence to make sure it is parallel to the blade. To reset the fence to the original setting, I just pop the jig into place and slide and lock the rip fence against it.

—GEORGE S. GRAHAM, *Branford, Fla.*

Extension Fence Helps Straighten Crooked Stock

I PUT OFF BUILDING ONE of those carriage fixtures for straightening crooked-edged boards for several years. The fixtures require expensive hold-down clamps, and they reduce the possible depth of cut by holding the workpiece off the saw table. The real problem was that the length of the regular rip fence is too short.

Then I noticed an 8-ft.-long piece of aluminum channel leaning in the corner of my shop. I clamped the channel to the rip fence, as shown, to produce an auxiliary fence that would guide fairly long stock in a straight line. To use the auxiliary fence, I just put the concave side of the board against the long fence and push it through. It works.

—WILLIAM MONDT, *San Diego, Calif.*

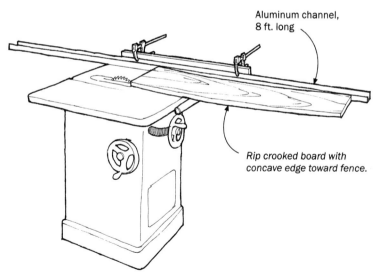

Aluminum channel,
8 ft. long

Rip crooked board with
concave edge toward fence.

20-ft. Tablesaw Fence

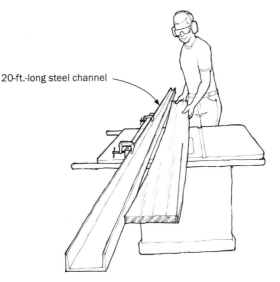

20-ft.-long steel channel

WHEN FACED WITH THE TASK OF STRAIGHTENING the warped edges on several hundred feet of 12-ft.-long 1x12 stock (for an order of baseboard), I remembered seeing a straight 20-ft.-long piece of steel channel, ¼ in. thick, at a local metal shop. Without a second thought, I went back to that shop and left with the channel on the roof of my pickup.

I clamp the channel to my existing rip fence as shown above and run the concave edge of the board against the fence so that only the ends touch the long fence. After I've ripped one edge of all of the stock, I remove the auxiliary fence and rip the other edge of the lumber using the regular fence. In my shop, most stock now passes through this low-cost, very efficient, straight ripping process right after planing. I store the fence overhead on two plywood hooks. I can lower my new 50-lb. helper onto the saw table one end at a time.

—MIKE McKENNA, *Ayer's Cliff, Que., Canada*

Tablesaw Extension Fence

THIS WOODEN EXTENSION FENCE slips over the tablesaw's regular fence and more than doubles its length. It is an indispensable accessory when extended contact with the rip fence is necessary. Mine is sized to fit my tablesaw's Biesemeyer fence, but the concept could be adapted to other rip-fence designs.

To make the fence, build a U-shaped channel that fits neatly over the rip fence. Add pieces to close off both ends. Add baffles on the inside for strength and to lock the extension in place over the rip fence. Assemble the extension with glue and plenty of screws. I cut an access opening directly above the locking lever of the rip fence so that I can operate it from above or below. Two coats of varnish will protect the fence for years. To use the extension, just slip it over the regular fence when you need it. Add an outfeed table at the back to support the extension fence and the workpiece.

—DICK DORN, *Oelwein, Iowa*

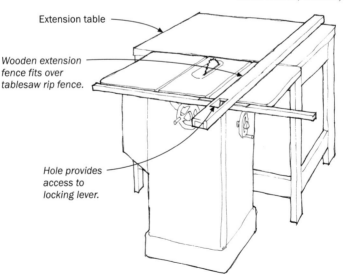

Extension table

Wooden extension fence fits over tablesaw rip fence.

Hole provides access to locking lever.

Micro-Adjustment Fixture for the Saw Fence

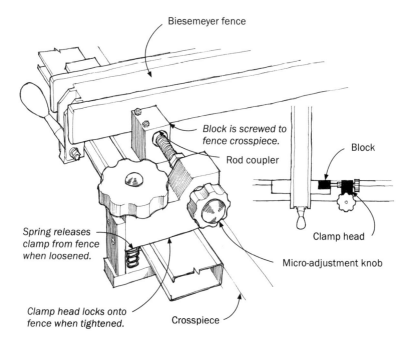

Biesemeyer fence

Block is screwed to
fence crosspiece.

Rod coupler

Block

Spring releases
clamp from fence
when loosened.

Clamp head

Micro-adjustment knob

Clamp head locks onto
fence when tightened.

Crosspiece

T HIS MICRO-ADJUSTMENT FIXTURE ENABLES you to fine-tune
the settings on a Biesemeyer-style tablesaw rip fence. The
fixture consists of two main parts: a block that attaches to the crosspiece of the rip fence and a clamp head that locks onto the front rail
of the fence.

The adjusting device itself is a 6-in.-long, ½-in. carriage bolt with a
wooden knob glued to its head with epoxy. The bolt runs through a
slightly oversized hole in the clamp head and into a rod coupler that
has been press-fit into the block. The length of the rod coupler, as
opposed to a standard hex nut, helps prevent the adjusting bolt from
binding as it is turned. The range of adjustment is about 1 in., more
than enough for most applications.

To use the device, leave the fence-locking lever up, and then clamp the head to the fence. Twist the micro-adjustment knob as necessary to locate the fence where you want it. Then lock the fence in place with the regular locking lever. The whole setup works smoothly and is a pleasure to use.

—TIMOTHY D. ANDERSON, *Chippewa Falls, Wisc.*

Add a Support to Rip Thin Plywood

WHEN RIPPING WIDE PANELS from thin sheet stock or plastic laminate, the edge next to the fence has a tendency to slip under the fence, which can be dangerous. To remedy this situation, clamp a piece of scrap under the fence, as shown.

—EDMOND VALADE, *Goffstown, N.H.*

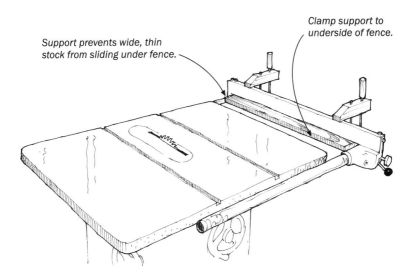

Clamp support to underside of fence.

Support prevents wide, thin stock from sliding under fence.

Micro-Adjustable Auxiliary Fence

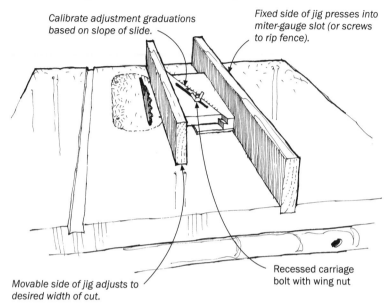

Calibrate adjustment graduations based on slope of slide.

Fixed side of jig presses into miter-gauge slot (or screws to rip fence).

Movable side of jig adjusts to desired width of cut.

Recessed carriage bolt with wing nut

I N THE PAST WHEN I WANTED TO ADJUST the width of a cut just a
hair, I usually just bumped the tablesaw fence with my hand—with
unpredictable results. To make my fence more precisely adjustable, I
designed this auxiliary fence based on the principle of a machinist's
parallel. The jig produces accurate and repeatable results, is easy to
build and is adaptable for all kinds of power saws and router tables.
The jig's dimensions and hardware can be chosen to suit the machine
and job requirements. I used a 9° angle on the slide. Although the
half-dovetail slide is not required, it does help hold the parts together.

You can attach the auxiliary fence to a tablesaw in two ways: Screw
it to an existing rip fence, or press it into the miter-gauge slot, as
shown. Although fastening the auxiliary fence to the rip fence gives a
wide range of adjustment, the advantage of pressing the fence into the

miter slot is that the unit can be removed while other work is being performed. Later, the auxiliary fence can be replaced with its setting undisturbed.

—BOYD EWING, *Depew, N.Y.*

Hanging Rip Fence

REMOVING AND THEN REINSTALLING the rip fence from my saw each time I crosscut a long board was time-consuming and awkward. My solution was to cut a couple inches off the rear rip-fence guide to allow the fence to hang from the front guide. After making the crosscut, I simply swing the fence up, and reinstall it on the rear guide.

—R. COADY, *Picton, Ont., Canada*

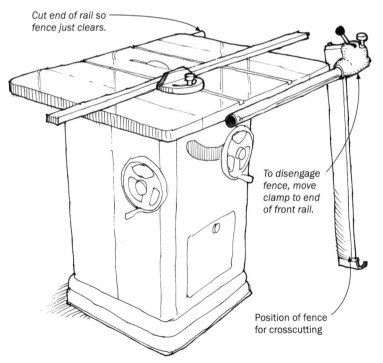

Cut end of rail so fence just clears.

To disengage fence, move clamp to end of front rail.

Position of fence for crosscutting

Rip-Fence Extensions, Two Ways

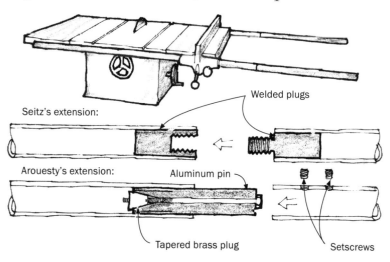

Welded plugs

Seitz's extension:

Arouesty's extension:

Aluminum pin

Tapered brass plug

Setscrews

M Y DECISION TO EXTEND the rip-fence rails on my Rockwell contractor's tablesaw came after a 4x8 sheet of plywood I was cutting "freehand" kicked back on me. I removed the tubular rails, took them to a machinist, and asked him to extend them so I could easily set the fence up to 48 in. The machinist welded a 2-in. steel plug in the end of each rail, drilled a ¾-in. hole through the plug, then tapped the hole with a coarse thread. He made the 24-in. extensions from tubular steel the same size as the rails and fitted each extension with a thread that screws into the plug in the original rails. These extensions have saved me countless hours of production time.

—STEPHEN SEITZ, *Oleyo, N.Y.*

T O EXTEND THE RAILS on my Rockwell tablesaw, I purchased a second set of tubular rails and devised expanding aluminum pins to attach them to the original rails. I drilled a bolt hole through the length of each pin and slotted the inner end, as shown in the sketch, so it could expand to lock the pin in the rail. With the pins locked into the original rails, I slip the spare rails on and fasten them in place with setscrews; the screws are located on the inside so they'll clear the rip fence.

I'm pleased with this system because I can remove the rails when they're not in use, and I can use the saw's racking micro-adjustment mechanism all the way across.

—RAYMOND AROUESTY, *Reseda, Calif.*

Miter-Gauge Setting Jig

SOME TABLESAW MITER-GAUGE SETTINGS are the result of tedious trial-and-error, cut-and-fit procedures. Here's how to preserve that hard-won setting for future use. Cut two lx2 strips about 1 ft. long. Clamp one to the bar and one to the gauge face. Glue and clamp the strips where they overlap. Reinforce this joint with a couple of screws or dowel pins. When the glue has cured, you can reproduce the setting anytime you like simply by pushing the jig against the gauge.

—TIM RODEGHIER, *Highland, Ind.*

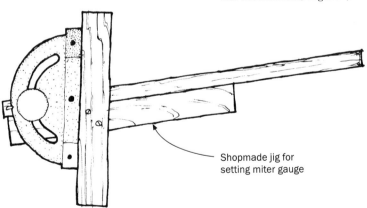

Shopmade jig for setting miter gauge

Miter-Gauge Alignment Fixture

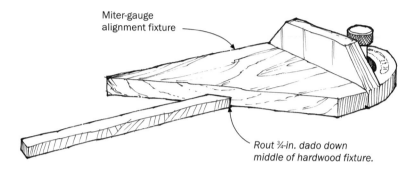

Miter-gauge
alignment fixture

Rout ¾-in. dado down
middle of hardwood fixture.

Y EARS AGO, I READ THAT YOU COULD EASILY adjust a miter gauge
to 90° by turning the gauge upside down, pushing it into the
tablesaw slot and tightening the bar. Perhaps this method works on
some saws but not on mine.

As an alternative, I built a hardwood alignment fixture slightly
wider than my miter gauge. I routed a ¾-in. slot down the middle
underside of the fixture to fit the miter-gauge bar. With the help of a
square and a plastic triangle, I cut one end of the fixture to a perfect
90° and the other end to a perfect 45°. I've since added a second fixture for 30° and 60°. To adjust the miter gauge, I place the fixture, slot
down, on the miter-gauge bar and tighten the face to the setting. It's
fast and accurate.

—CLYDE HUNTER, JR., *San Jose, Calif.*

Sliding Miter-Gauge Fence

I ADDED A SLIDING FENCE TO MY TABLESAW'S miter gauge to enable it to perform like the gauges found on many European power tools. With a sliding fence, you can move the end of the fence right next to the blade for a 45° miter cut, then reposition it for a 90° cut. I made the miter fence from a piece of maple, metal track and T-bolts made specifically for jigs by Rockler Woodworking and Hardware (4365 Willow Dr., Medina, MN. 55340; 800-279-4441; www.rockler.com). Wing nuts with toothed washers lock the fence in position.

—DON CARKHUFF, *Darien, Ill.*

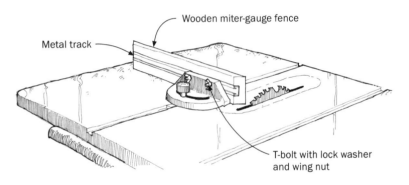

Wooden miter-gauge fence

Metal track

T-bolt with lock washer and wing nut

Preventing Miter-Gauge Creep

TO PREVENT WORK FROM slipping and creeping, glue sandpaper (with contact cement) to the face of your tablesaw's miter gauge.

—DEAN CHASE, *Nevada City, Calif.*

Eliminating Miter-Gauge Side Play

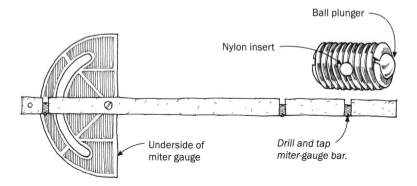

Ball plunger

Nylon insert

Underside of
miter gauge

Drill and tap
miter-gauge bar.

H ERE'S A WAY TO ELIMINATE miter-gauge side play. This inexpensive method uses ball-plunger screws inserted transversely to the bar at three locations. The plungers are threaded steel inserts fitted with spring-loaded stainless-steel balls. I use the heavy force plungers (2 to 5 lbs. end force), 10-32 threads, ½ in. long, with a nylon locking element (available from MSC Industrial Supply Co., 151 Sunnyside Blvd., Plainview, NY 11803-1592). Drill three holes through the bar—two near the tip and one near the base—and tap for the threads. Screw the plungers into the holes with the balls facing the same direction. Use a screwdriver to adjust the plunger depth until all side play is removed without excessive friction or interference. The plunging action of the balls will compensate for any variations in the saw table's slot width.

—RICHARD SHULTZ, *Cinnaminson, N.J.*

Enhanced Tablesaw Miter Gauge

F OR FIVE YEARS I HAVE LOOKED UNSUCCESSFULLY for a 10-in. tablesaw with a "rolling table" facility for crosscuts and miters. The one I'm familiar with is a big, old Oliver. The new Rockwell and Powermatic sliding-table attachments are similar in concept and are fine if you have $2,000 to spend on the saw and rig. They take up room on the left of the saw and are really designed for the large stock requirements of a cabinet shop. There are plywood jigs that sit atop the saw and serve the purpose, but I've found them to be inaccurate. My solution is simple, inexpensive and as effective as the expensive attachments if you are not cutting whole sheets of plywood.

Simply take your miter gauge apart and insert a piece of Formica between the miter-gauge bar and the protractor fence. Cut the Formica the same size as the left half of the table, and fasten the smooth side down. When using the fixture, you can press down on the piece of wood being crosscut without causing the wood to bind as it slides on the table. The Formica spreads the pressure over a wider area. The addition of a backboard faced with abrasive paper practically eliminates creep.

—MICHAEL J. HANLEY, *Cedarburg, Wisc.*

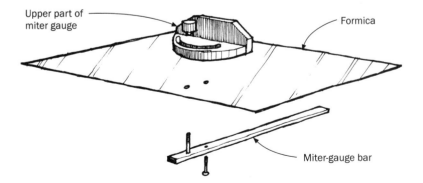

Upper part of miter gauge

Formica

Miter-gauge bar

Remedy for a Worn Miter Gauge

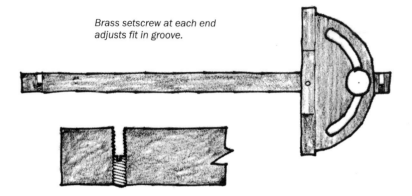

Brass setscrew at each end
adjusts fit in groove.

HERE'S A BETTER WAY TO TAKE OUT THE SLOP in a loose or worn miter-gauge rail. It's certainly a more elegant solution than peening the rail. First, dismantle the gauge. Drill and tap a hole across each end of the rail bar to accept a ¼-in. setscrew. I make my own brass setscrews by cutting the head off a brass bolt and hacksawing a screw slot. Install the setscrews in the bar, and adjust them until the rail fits the slot perfectly.

—HARRIE E. BURNELL, *Newburyport, Mass.*

Improved Miter-Gauge Runner

OVER THE YEARS, I'VE SEEN MANY PLANS for homemade jigs that utilize a hardwood runner that fits in the miter-gauge slot. But because wood shrinks and expands depending on the humidity, the runner's fit and hence the jig's accuracy will vary. To correct the problem, cut the runner a bit undersize so that it is loose in the slot. Then install four ½-in.-long brass screws in countersunk holes along one edge of the runner. You can adjust the screws to get a perfect fit, regardless of the humidity. The brass screws won't wear the sides of the slot and are easily replaced if they wear out.

—LARRY LOO, M.D., *Clovis, Calif.*

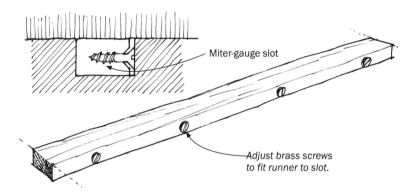

Miter-gauge slot

Adjust brass screws to fit runner to slot.

Expanding the Range of a Miter Gauge

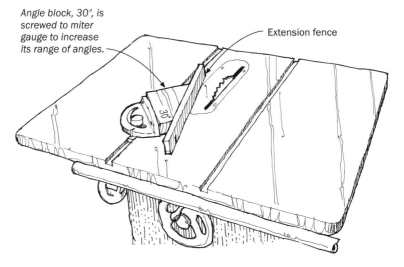

Angle block, 30°, is screwed to miter gauge to increase its range of angles.

Extension fence

S OME OF MY PROJECTS REQUIRE CUTS at 12° or 15°, but my table-saw's miter gauge is limited to 30° to the left or right of the 90° setting. To expand its range, I made an adapter that I screw to the face of the miter gauge. The adapter is a 2-in.-thick block of wood cut at 30°, which allows me to make acute angle cuts down to 0°. The block can be reversed on the gauge for use in the right-hand miter-gauge slot. Adding an extension fence to the block is also helpful in many situations and lets you hold long workpieces so your fingers aren't near the blade. But don't attempt to hold small pieces with your hand while cutting steep acute angles.

—KENNETH WOLFE, *Wausaukee, Wisc.*

Adjustable Miter-Gauge Stop

HERE IS A JIG THAT'S EASY AND FAST to make and to use. It's basically a stick with a dowel through it, clamped to the table-saw miter gauge to give precise production-run cutoffs. It works at any angle.

—ALAN MILLER, *Lakewood, Colo.*

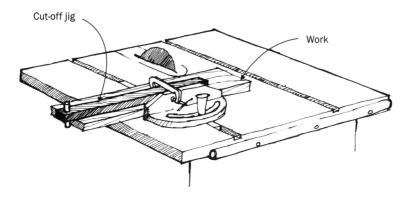

Cut-off jig

Work

Stop Block from a Magnet

A MAGNET FROM A JUNKED RADIO SPEAKER makes an excellent stop block on the tablesaw. Just plop the strong magnet where needed. The magnets require no clamps and are infinitely adjustable.

—R. A. BOLSTER, *Ashland, Ore.*

Magnetic Duplicate Cut-Off Aid

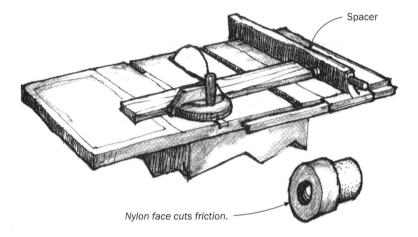

Spacer

Nylon face cuts friction.

THIS GADGET HAS SAVED ME A LOT of time when cutting duplicate lengths on the tablesaw. It's a spacer that ensures clearance between the cutoff stock and the rip fence, thereby avoiding the danger of kickback. My spacer is simply a round magnet with a threaded hole through it. These magnets should be standard items at your local hardware store or five-and-dime. Screw a short length of nylon rod or other slippery alternative to the magnet, and cut the unit to exactly 1 in. in length.

To use, just pop it on the rip fence, set the fence to the desired dimension plus 1 in., butt your stock against it and cut. Best of all, the spacer is always handy—stuck on the back side of the fence.

—RICHARD BOLMER, *Anaheim, Calif.*

A Safer Stop Block for Cut-Off Work

YOU MIGHT FILE THIS UNDER THE "what happened?" heading. I was making multiple crosscuts on a tablesaw with a miter gauge, using a 1-in. standoff (acting as a stop block) clamped to the rip fence. I had done it this way many times without incident. Anyway, I was cutting 5-in.-long blocks from 3-in.-wide stock. While removing a cutoff, I must have moved it in a twisting motion, so it touched the blade. The stock briefly jammed between the fence and blade. The block bounced off me and drove itself into the wall behind me. Re-creating the accident, I found the diagonal measure of the piece exceeded the distance between the fence and the blade. Jammo-whammo.

So I made a 3-in.-wide standoff for the fence. It's nothing fancy: just two pieces of scrap—one vertical, one horizontal. I made it exactly 3 in. wide, so I can clamp it to the fence and then set the fence 3 in. beyond the length desired. Now there is plenty of room to remove stock. There has been no repeat incident.

—JIM WRIGHT, *Berkley, Mass.*

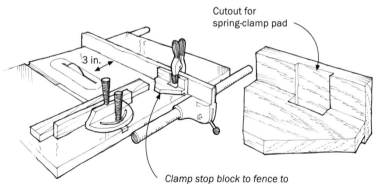

Cutout for
spring-clamp pad

3 in.

Clamp stop block to fence to
reduce potential for kickback.

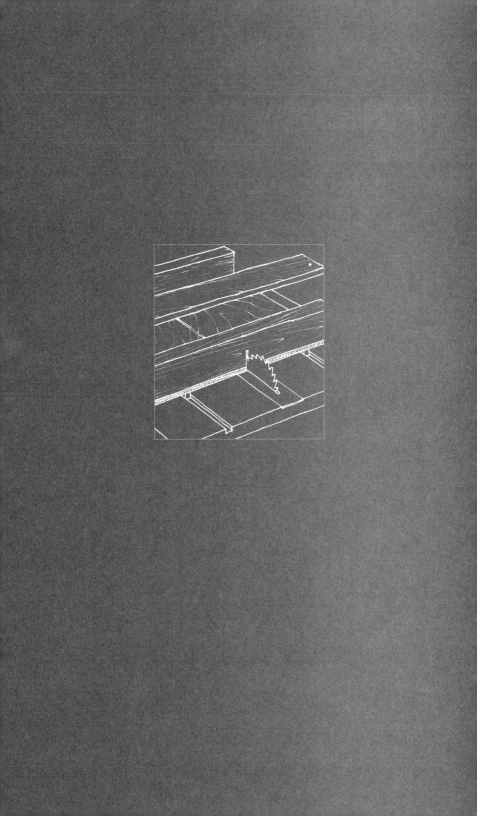

Chapter 9

CROSSCUTTING
&
MITERING
FIXTURES

Sliding Tablesaw Carriage

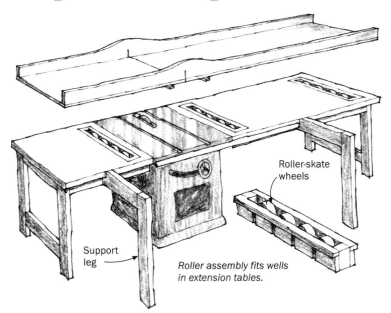

Roller-skate wheels

Support leg

Roller assembly fits wells in extension tables.

I F YOU'VE EVER ATTEMPTED to crosscut a 6-ft.-long, 2-ft.-wide panel on the tablesaw, you know the operation is awkward, error-prone and even scary. By contrast, when you add the sliding carriage described here, tablesaw crosscutting is made more accurate, faster and safer. The fixture is straightforward with two main components: an auxiliary bed fitted with rollers made from skate wheels, and a sliding carriage that rolls atop the bed, using the miter-gauge slots as a track.

The auxiliary bed fitted with rollers is really the key to the fixture. Without the rollers the heavy sliding carriage would stick and bind. To make the auxiliary bed, first construct two outrigger tables to bolt up to the saw as shown. The size of the tables is your choice, of course, but I recommend that the tables-plus-saw add up to at least 8 ft. long. The rollers are made up in three box frames, each containing four nylon roller skate wheels mounted on ¼-in. threaded-rod axles. The roller boxes drop into wells in the top of each outrigger table as shown. The boxes pop out when they are not in use and can be replaced by plain plywood inserts. It is a good idea to design in some sort of height adjustment for the rollers in case they are too low or too high in use.

The sliding carriage is nothing more than a large panel of plywood with fences fixed to the front and the back edges. Waxed maple runners screwed to the bottom of the carriage slide in the miter-gauge slots and ensure the table tracks at right angles to the blade. I bolted the fences to the panel using slotted holes so that I could adjust the fences for a perfectly square cut.

Because the sliding table is heavy, another necessary component of the fixture is a support stand to hold the table when it's pulled back toward the operator before the cut. You may choose to incorporate this support into the design of the auxiliary bed. In my case I made up a couple of removable legs I can fasten in place whenever I use the sliding table.

Another benefit of the fixture is that you can use the roller feature without the sliding carriage. The rollers make ripping a full sheet of plywood a breeze.

—BILL AMAYA, *Hailey, Ind.*

Cutoff Box

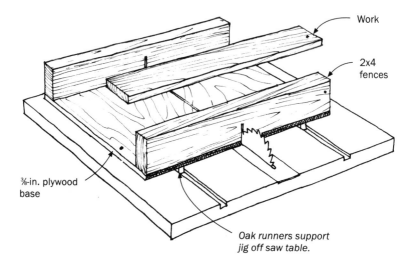

Work

2x4 fences

⅜-in. plywood base

Oak runners support jig off saw table.

T HIS EASY-TO-BUILD BOX is superior to the miter gauge for simple 90° cutoff work on the tablesaw. Right-angle accuracy is built into the fixture; there's no adjustment necessary. Also, because the work is supported on both sides of the cut, there is none of the creeping that plagues cutoff work with the miter gauge.

Although the size of the fixture is variable, I suggest you make it just a little smaller than the tablesaw top. For a typical saw, this will give you room to handle work that's 18 in. to 24 in. wide. Make the bed from ⅜-in. plywood and the fences from 2x4s. Glue and screw the fences to the bed (avoid putting a screw in the path of the blade). Cut the oak runners so that they slide easily in the miter-gauge tracks and support the bed about ¼ in. off the table. Be very accurate in attaching the runners and you'll always get a square cut.

—JON GULLETT, *Washington, Ill.*

Safer Sliding Cutoff Box

A SLIDING CROSSCUT BOX IS A big help when working with small pieces of stock on a tablesaw. The problem is that the sawblade emerges suddenly from the rear of the box at the end of a stroke just where your fingers could be. This hazard is greatly reduced by adding a hard maple guard (I painted mine red) to the jig where the blade emerges. When the jig is at the end of its stroke, the blade is still safely within the maple block. My guard is held by screws through the back fence. I also added a Plexiglas shield over the blade.

—MICHAEL A. COVINGTON, *Athens, Ga.*

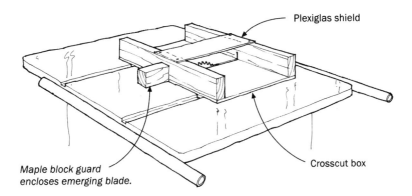

Plexiglas shield

Maple block guard
encloses emerging blade.

Crosscut box

Ball-Bearing Guides
for Tablesaw Cutoff Box

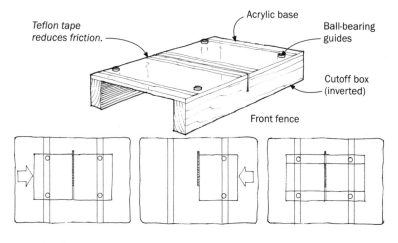

Teflon tape reduces friction.

Acrylic base

Ball-bearing guides

Cutoff box (inverted)

Front fence

1. Push left two bearings against right side of miter-gauge slot. Cut base in two.

2. Push right side of base to left so bearings contact left side of slot, and cut again.

3. Clamp halves of base together, and attach fences.

THE WOODEN PUZZLES I make require safe, accurate cuts of small pieces of wood. That's why I designed this cutoff box that uses ball-bearing guides, an acrylic base and Teflon tape.

Start with a 12-in. by 24-in. piece of ½-in.-thick acrylic. Drill four holes, and install bolts for bearing axles. Space the axles in pairs at a distance equal to the center-to-center spacing of your saw's miter-gauge slots. The bearings don't need to be precisely located at this stage.

With the bearings mounted, flip the base so the bearings are in the saw's miter slots. Push the acrylic base to the right to cause the two left-hand bearings to contact the right edge of the left miter-gauge slot. Saw the base in half. Repeat this step for the right half of the base, but this time push it left so that its two bearings contact the left side of the saw's right miter-gauge slot. You now have two pieces of acrylic separated by a saw kerf when the bearings are against the inboard edges of the miter-gauge slots.

Attach the front and back fences to the base using 4-in.-long bolts and washers in oversized holes to provide adjustment. Hold the base on the saw table with bar clamps while you're attaching the fences so you locate the bearings properly. To complete the box, add strips of Teflon tape to the underside of the acrylic base along both sides of the saw kerf and outside of each miter-gauge slot.

Use quick-action clamps to hold workpieces safely in place during cuts. Be careful that you don't push the box too far past the blade because the box will lose lateral stability. However, stops clamped to the back side of the saw will prevent the bearings from coming out of the miter-gauge slots.

—WAYNE DANIEL, *Minden, Nev.*

Squaring the Fence
on a Tablesaw Cutoff Box

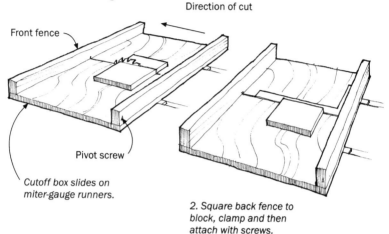

1. Attach squaring block, and then raise sawblade through it.

Direction of cut

Front fence

Pivot screw

Cutoff box slides on miter-gauge runners.

2. Square back fence to block, clamp and then attach with screws.

I'VE FOUND AN EASY WAY TO SET THE BACK FENCE on a tablesaw cutoff box perfectly square to the cut line: Build the cutoff box to the dimensions you need, attach rails to run in the tablesaw miter-gauge slots and attach the front fence securely to the box. (The front fence is the one farthest away from you when you're using the saw.) Attach the back fence with one wood screw through the bottom in the left corner to allow the fence to pivot.

Now attach a piece of scrap wood near the back fence with double-faced tape. This will be used as a squaring block. Raise the sawblade through the bottom of the cutoff box, and cut through the squaring block but not through the back fence. Remove half of the squaring block, and pivot the back fence until it is square to the remaining squaring block. Use an accurate framing square for this. Clamp the back fence in place, and attach it with screws through the bottom. Remove what's left of the squaring block and you're set.

—TONY BUSCH, *Port Orchard, Wash.*

Improved Miter-Slot Runners

With runners in slots, square table to slots, and glue down.

Pennies elevate runners during glue-up.

ANYONE WHO HAS EVER TRIED TO MAKE a sliding table for a tablesaw knows that correctly aligning the runners to the sliding table can be frustrating. The trick is to do it in place. This drastically simplifies the process and virtually ensures a perfect fit and smooth sliding action.

First cut and fit runners for the miter-gauge slots. Make the runners a little shorter than the total length of the slot and slightly thinner than the depth of the slot. The runners should be hardwood (red oak or hard maple is a good choice). Sand or plane the runners until they move freely but snugly. The runner size typically will be ¾ in. wide by a little less than ⅜ in. thick. The runners should not touch the bottom of the slots when the table is finished.

Attach the sliding table to the runners. The runners should be elevated until they are just proud of the table surface. I use pennies for this, evenly distributing four or five stacks of two pennies along the bottom of each slot to raise the runners.

Align the ends of the runners with the front ends of the slots, and shim or wedge the runners to force them to the edge of the miter slot closest to the blade. This removes any remaining slop. Apply glue to the top of the runners, and carefully set the sliding table on top, aligning the front edge of the table at 90° to the miter slots. Finally, add weight to the top of the table over the runners for a good glue bond. I generally use a good stack of bricks.

After the glue has cured, remove the sliding table, pennies and shims from the saw. For insurance, screw the runners to the table from below, countersinking the heads. Apply a coat or two of paste wax to the table bottom and runners, and you'll be in sliding heaven.

—MIKE SMITH, *Smyrna, Ga.*

Board-Straightening Fixture

THIS IS A GREAT BOARD-STRAIGHTENING FIXTURE. Simply press one end of the crooked board into the nail at the head of the fixture, allowing the board to overhang the plywood base by ½ in. or so. Hold the board on the sandpaper strips so it won't move, and slide the whole arrangement through the tablesaw with the wood runner in the miter-gauge slot. You can straighten a dozen boards in five minutes.

—JIM PUTERBAUGH, *Portland, Ore.*

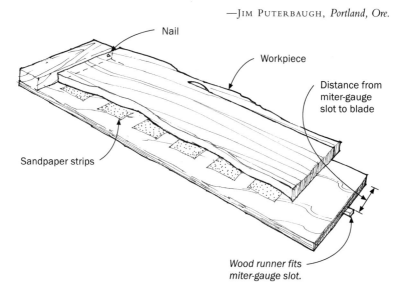

Nail

Workpiece

Distance from miter-gauge slot to blade

Sandpaper strips

Wood runner fits miter-gauge slot.

Cutting Wide Panels

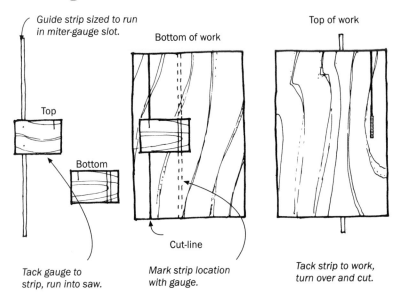

Guide strip sized to run in miter-gauge slot.

Bottom of work

Top of work

Top

Bottom

Cut-line

Tack gauge to strip, run into saw.

Mark strip location with gauge.

Tack strip to work, turn over and cut.

A SIMPLE WOODEN STRIP TACKED to the bottom of the workpiece will let you rip panels that are too wide for the rip fence on your tablesaw. Size the wooden strip to run in the miter-gauge slot (generally ¾ in. by ⅜ in.), and cut it slightly longer than the cut to be made. To lay out the strip's location on the workpiece, I used a small piece of ⅛-in.-thick birch plywood as a distance gauge. Tack the plywood to the strip, then run the assembly into the saw for about an inch. Turn the assembly over, and mark the strip's location on the plywood with a pencil line on both sides of the strip. Remove the plywood, and you have a gauge that shows the exact relation of table slot to saw kerf.

To use the strip, draw an accurate cut line on the back of the work. Now use the distance gauge to lay out the strip location, and brad the strip to the bottom of the work. Remember to position the strip so that the saw kerf is to the waste side of the cut line. Turn the assembly over, feed the strip into the table slot and make the cut. If you have done the layout carefully, the cut will be right on. I use a thin-rim plywood blade, which, since the finished side of the work is up, produces a smooth, clean cut.

The procedure is not practical for the first cut on a 4x8 sheet of plywood or for quantity cutting. But it works fine for those 30-in. and 36-in. panels that are so awkward to cut on a small saw.

—WILLIAM LANGDON, *Lake Forest, Ill.*

Crosscutting Wide Panels

HERE IS AN ACCURATE AND SIMPLE WAY to crosscut plywood panels or boards that are too wide to cut using the saw's miter gauge. Start with a straight 1x2 longer than the panel is wide. Clamp the 1x2 underneath the panel so that it becomes a fence that runs against the saw table's edge. Carefully measure and position the fence using a framing square. Then clamp the new fence to the panel with C-clamps. The method can be adapted to ripping plywood and wall paneling by lengthening the fence. By clamping the fence to wide panels at an angle, you can make miter cuts that are virtually impossible any other way.

—STEVE DELAY, *Hollister, Calif.*

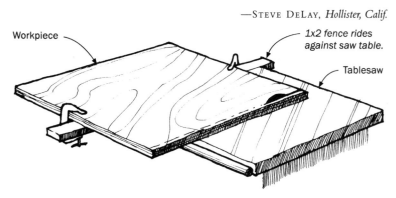

Workpiece

1x2 fence rides against saw table.

Tablesaw

Cutting Small Parts on the Tablesaw

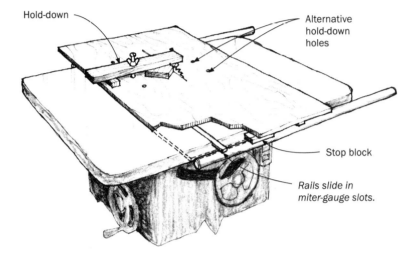

Hold-down

Alternative hold-down holes

Stop block

Rails slide in miter-gauge slots.

I MADE THIS FIXTURE TO CUT PARTS for small models and miniature furniture. It works so accurately and safely that I cut even
conventional-size parts with it instead of using the miter gauge.

The fixture is made from a piece of plywood that is 8 in. to 14 in.
longer than the table, depending on the length of cuts you plan to
make. Screw hardwood runners underneath the plywood to slide in
the miter-gauge slots, and screw stop blocks at both ends of the underside to prevent accidentally cutting the fixture in two. With the fixture
in place, raise the blade through it to cut the blade slot.

Drill several hold-down anchor holes through the plywood, and install ⅜-in. T-nuts underneath. I have various anchor locations on my
fixture to suit my individual operations. A small wood scrap will serve
as a hold-down. Bore a hole through it for a ⅜-in. bolt, and thread a
wing nut over the bolt before putting it through the wood block.
Place the workpiece under the hold-down near the blade, and place a

block the same thickness as the workpiece at the other end of the hold-down; just tighten down on the wing nut to hold the workpiece in place.

I've found the hold-down applies enough force to lock the workpiece in place in just about any cutting operation, and my hands never come near the moving blade.

—DON H. ANDERSON, *Sequim, Wash.*

Mitering Jig with a Holding Block

I USE A TABLESAW MITER JIG THAT INCLUDES a holding block in a channel to press the work against the fence. Be sure to cut the holding block large enough to secure the stock against the fence and to keep your fingers away from the blade.

—JOHN C. ORT, *Portsmouth, R.I.*

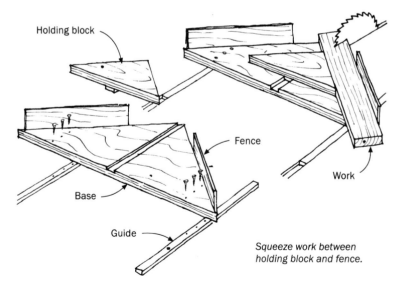

Holding block

Fence

Work

Base

Guide

Squeeze work between holding block and fence.

Mitering Frames on the Tablesaw

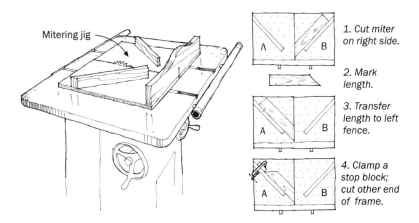

Mitering jig

1. Cut miter on right side.

2. Mark length.

3. Transfer length to left fence.

4. Clamp a stop block; cut other end of frame.

MUCH OF THE FURNITURE I MAKE is based on mitered frames, which require corners that have to meet perfectly. To make these frames, I use a sliding table jig on my tablesaw. The jig is simple to build, ideal to clamp work to and easily allows mitered workpiece corners to be marked for length.

Start with a piece of ½-in. plywood fitted with two rails on the bottom to fit in the tablesaw's miter-gauge slots and a fence at the back tall enough so it won't get sawed through. Place the fixture on the saw, and saw a kerf from front to back using the blade you will use for mitering. Now attach the left fence (fence A) to the base using a 45° triangle registered against the saw kerf to establish the angle. Attach the right fence (fence B) using a framing square set against fence A. Leave enough space between the tall fence and the angled fences for a typical frame workpiece. Also, for safety, make the throat between the fences wide.

To make a frame, first miter one end of all four pieces of the frame using fence B. Mark the required length on one of the workpieces, place the workpiece against fence A and transfer the measurement from the workpiece to the fence. Clamp a stop block at this location on fence A. Now miter the other end of all the pieces. When assembling the frame pieces, be sure to join A's to B's. Any slight error in the fences is negated by the 90° included angle, which ensures that each frame corner is perfectly square.

—David A. Saunders, *Manchester, Conn.*

Dual Crosscut and Mitering Fixture for the Radial-Arm Saw

B Y LEAVING A 4-IN. GAP between the fence and the 45° guides, boards can be cut to length, then shifted to the 45° guides for mitering. Without the gap, the boards can be cut to length only by using another saw or by removing the jig.

—M. B. Williams, *Potomac, Md.*

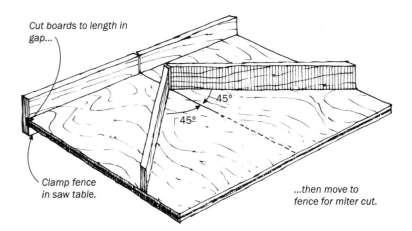

Cut boards to length in gap...

45°

45°

Clamp fence in saw table.

...then move to fence for miter cut.

Tablesaw Mitering Jig

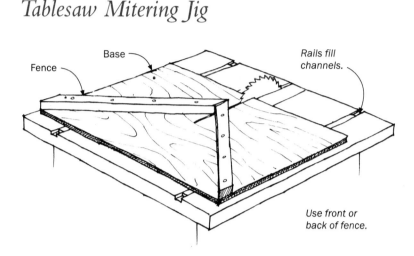

Fence

Base

Rails fill channels.

Use front or back of fence.

T HIS TABLESAW JIG HAS HELPED ME TO CUT ACCURATE miters
for 25 years. To make it, cut two table-length rails from well-
seasoned oak or hickory, and sand to a sliding fit in the miter-gauge
channels. With the rails in place in the channels, set the ½-in. plywood
base (cut a little smaller than the saw table) on the rails so that the
midpoint of the forward edge is aligned with the sawblade. Fasten the
base to the rails with ¾-in. flathead screws. Now slide the jig back,
raise the sawblade and saw into the jig 3 in. or so. From the center of
the kerf, extend the saw line to the back side of the jig. Mark two
lines 45° from the saw line with a draftsman's triangle, and fasten the
two 1-in.-wide fences on the lines with screws.

Ordinarily, I use the front edges of the fences to hold the pieces to
be cut. But to cut, say, the four pieces for a picture frame, cut the
pieces square to length plus twice the thickness of the saw kerf and
use the back edges of the jig fences. One fence aligns the work; the
other serves as a stop.

—BAYARD M. COLE, *Marietta, Ga.*

Miter-Gauge Rail Trick

THE NEXT TIME YOU BUILD A TABLESAW FIXTURE fitted with wood guide strips that run in the miter-gauge slots, cut small rabbets in the top edges of the guides. The rabbets not only eliminate glue cleanup, but they also make final fitting easier because you can handplane the edges of the strips without having to dig into hard-to-reach inside corners.

—TIM RODEGHIER, *Three Oaks, Mich.*

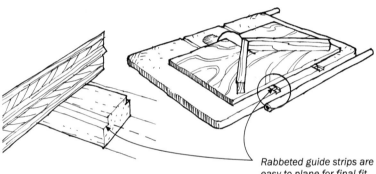

Rabbeted guide strips are
easy to plane for final fit.

Making Accurate Miter Cuts

I'VE OFTEN SEEN WOODWORKERS STRUGGLE to make miter cuts on a miter box. If you want accurate miters, I would definitely not use a miter box. For carpenter's work it's okay, but no miter boxes are accurate enough to cut a smooth joint. To make accurate miters you need a good 10-in. tablesaw with at least a 1-hp motor and an accurate miter jig.

—TAGE FRID, *from a question by Barbara Emley, San Francisco, Calif.*

Perfect Tablesaw Miters

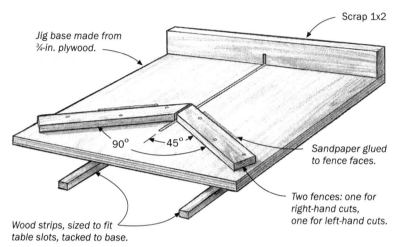

Scrap 1x2

Jig base made from ¾-in. plywood.

90°   45°

Wood strips, sized to fit table slots, tacked to base.

Sandpaper glued to fence faces.

Two fences: one for right-hand cuts, one for left-hand cuts.

THE BEST METHOD I'VE SEEN FOR CUTTING dead-on 45° miters on the tablesaw uses a simple plywood jig that has two fences: one for left-hand miters and one for right-hand miters. These fences are precisely oriented and fixed to a plywood base with runners that fit a tablesaw's miter slots. The workpiece is held against one of the fences and the jig pushed forward to make the cut.

To make the jig, start with a piece of ⅜-in.- or ¾-in.-thick plywood (particleboard is okay, but it's much heavier and not as strong), about the same size and shape as your saw table. If you are planning to cut some really wide or long pieces, you might want to make the base even larger. Now make two strips, sized to fit your miter slots exactly, and glue and tack them to the bottom of the base. Glue and screw a scrap 1x2 to the top back edge of the base. With the blade set to cut all the way through the plywood, slide the jig into the blade so that it cuts about halfway into the base.

To make the fences, cut two strips, each about 2½ in. wide, with 45° miters on the ends. Glue narrow strips of 120-grit sandpaper to the edges of the strips that end in the miter points. (The sandpaper will help keep the workpiece from slipping along the fence later.) Now butt the ends of the miter together, and use an accurate framing square to keep the strips square to one another. Place the miter over the saw kerf in the jig base, and carefully orient the fence assembly to a 45° angle to the line of cut (see drawing). Glue and screw the fences down; then slide the jig into the running sawblade just far enough to cut through the end of the fence miter.

To use the jig, first cut your frame parts to approximate length, and hold the parts firmly against one fence or the other while pushing the jig through the miter cut. By making sure all pairs of frame members are exactly the same length and by making right- and left-hand cuts using the two fences, you can be assured of always getting a perfectly square frame.

—SANDOR NAGYSZALANCZY,
from a question by Fletcher K. Wood, Kanab, Utah

Cleaning Up Miters on the Disk Sander

I THINK THAT A GOOD, CLEAN MITER JOINT is one of the hardest joints to make. A tablesaw is no better than the miter gauge that comes with it for making this joint, and your best bet might be to invest in a miter trimmer. A radial-arm saw probably does a better job than a tablesaw because the work doesn't drag on the saw table. I cut miters (when I have to) on the tablesaw, and then make the final adjustment on a disk sander set accurately to 45°. It may be cheating, but it works.

—SIMON WATTS,
from a question by Barbara Emley, San Francisco, Calif.

Trig Jig for Accurate Angles

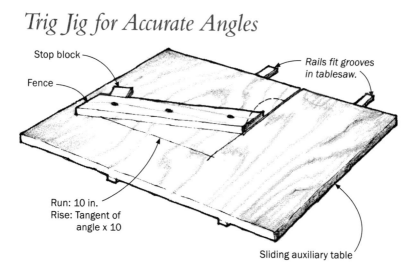

Stop block

Fence

Rails fit grooves in tablesaw.

Run: 10 in.
Rise: Tangent of angle x 10

Sliding auxiliary table

WITH THIS SIMPLE JIG AND A LITTLE TRIGONOMETRY, you can cut odd angles on the tablesaw more accurately than with the saw's miter gauge. First, construct a sliding table using two maple rails and a piece of ¾-in. plywood. To ensure perfect alignment, lay the rails in the saw's grooves and tack the plywood to them temporarily, then flop the plywood over and screw the rails down. Next, raise the sawblade and cut about halfway across the jig.

Trigonometry provides an easy and accurate method for laying out the angled fence. Find the tangent of the desired angle from a trigonometry table or with a pocket scientific calculator. The tangent gives you the ratio of the angle's vertical rise to its horizontal run. If your angle is 11.25°, for example, the tangent is 0.19891 (rounded to 0.2). Therefore, for each inch of horizontal run, the vertical rise is 0.2 in. To make layout easier, scale up the measurements by multiplying by 10. This results in a base horizontal line of 10 in. and a vertical rise of 2 in. Mark these measurements on the jig as shown in the sketch, and draw a line between the two points to locate the fence.

—ERIC SCHRAMM, *Los Gatos, Calif.*

Triangle Tips

A N ARCHITECT'S 45° TRIANGLE is inexpensive and handy around the shop. Attach a ½-in. by ½-in. strip of walnut along the hypotenuse with No. 2 R. H. brass wood screws to make a miter square. Take care not to cut into the edge of the triangle when you scribe with a metal instrument.

—DWIGHT G. GORRELL, *Centerville, Kans.*

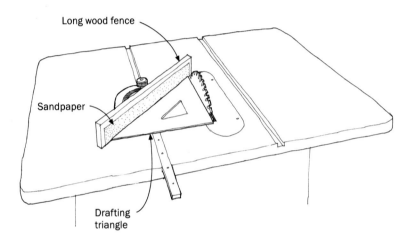

Long wood fence

Sandpaper

Drafting triangle

A N INEXPENSIVE BUT ACCURATE plastic drafting triangle gives a perfect 45° setting on the tablesaw. A long wood face on the fence with sandpaper attached prevents slippage and further improves accuracy.

—JIM RICHEY, *Houston, Tex.*

Double Miter-Gauge Jig for Cutting Angles

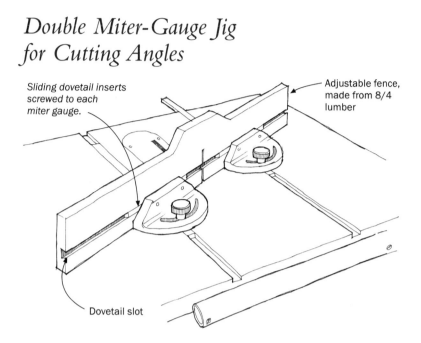

Sliding dovetail inserts screwed to each miter gauge.

Adjustable fence, made from 8/4 lumber

Dovetail slot

F RUSTRATED BY THE INACCURACIES and trial-and-error test cuts that seem to go with using a regular miter gauge on the tablesaw, I had set the gauge aside and relied on dozens of auxiliary fences preset to specific angles. But now, after years of not using that one miter gauge, I discovered all I really needed was two miter gauges connected by a hefty fence.

To make the jig, I set one miter gauge in each slot and screwed a 2-in.-thick oak fence—2 in. wider than the maximum height of the blade—to both of the gauges. To allow the fence to move slightly when the angle is changed, I cut a dovetailed slot, centered where the screw holes for the miter gauge go into the fence. Then I made some mating dovetail pieces, slid them in the dovetail slot and added screws through the miter gauges into the mating pieces.

With the jig, I can measure the cut angle directly between the fence and the blade and hold angles more accurately. When I need to cut a complementary angle, I simply slide the workpiece along the fence and make a cut on the other side of the blade.

—JOSEPH M. SANTAPAU, *Yardley, Pa.*

Cutting Perfect Miters on the Tablesaw

WHEN TRYING TO RIP BEVELED MITERS or crosscut perfect miters on a tablesaw, the 45° blade setting is usually anything but 45°. And if the angle is off even a little, the cumulative error makes that fourth corner gap in your assembly very noticeable. Here's how to ensure virtually perfect miters. Buy two 45° plastic drafting triangles, one clear and one colored (for better visibility), and set them up on the blade as shown. You will only be able to get about 3 in. of the triangle down on the blade, but this should be enough. Hold the second triangle on the saw table, or clamp it between two pieces of scrap. Adjust the blade until the gap is even; the long bases of the triangles exaggerate the gap.

—JAMES H. WOLFE, *Enumclaw, Wash.*

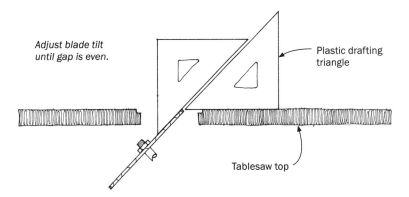

Adjust blade tilt until gap is even.

Plastic drafting triangle

Tablesaw top

Mitered Box Jig

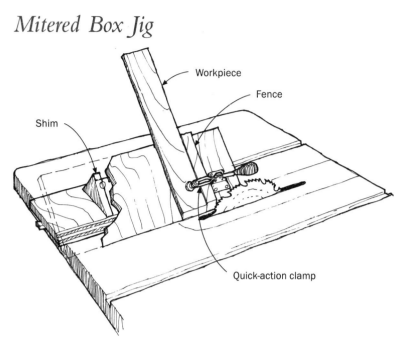

Workpiece

Fence

Shim

Quick-action clamp

WHEN MAKING SMALL BOXES WITH MITERED CORNERS, I find it very time-consuming to set the tablesaw to the required dead-accurate 45° cut. Hence, I made this little jig, and with it, I can cut the miters quickly, accurately and, most of all, safely—and with the blade set at 90°. Make the base and slanted platform from seven-ply birch plywood. Cut the two inside supports as close as possible to 45° on the tablesaw. Fasten these two supports to the base with screws and glue. Then, attach the slanted platform to the supports, but do not glue them and use only one screw. This will allow you to shim the slanted platform to fine-tune the angle later if needed. Screw a vertical fence onto the slanted platform—square to the platform's long edge—and a guide rail to the bottom of the base to run in the saw's miter gauge slot. Finish the jig with two or three coats of polyurethane to repel moisture. Finally, screw an adjustable, quick-action clamp to the jig to hold the material firmly during the cut. This clamp is essential. For safety's sake, do not attempt to use the jig without it.

To calibrate the jig, make a trial cut with scrap lumber and check it with a 45° square. Adjust the platform with shims between the supports and the slanted platform until the cut is exact. For even finer tuning, cut four identical pieces and miter all their ends. Assemble the four pieces to ensure all four corners are dead on. If not, shim the platform again, this time with thin paper. Tighten both screws the same amount each time.

Now you're ready to make boxes. I use masking tape to roll the box together, both for trying the fit and also for holding the corners while the glue sets.

—KEN WALL, *Sand Springs, Okla.*

Two-Sided Miter Jig

I'D LIKE TO THANK KEN WALL, whose single-sided vertical miter jig (see previous page) inspired this double-sided version. I've found the two-sided jig is even better because its accuracy is permanently established by the slanted platforms mounted 90° from each other, not by the angle between the blade and the jig, which could change. If you cut one of the mitered pieces on the left side of the jig and the other on the right, they're sure to form a 90° angle. The jig has proved excellent for small boxes, frames and most trim.

To make the jig, start with a 20-in.-sq. plywood base. Attach hardwood runners to the underside to slide in the miter-gauge slots on either side of the blade. Mount the left platform to the base at a 45° angle. Then mount the right platform using a large framing square and shims to place it at a perfect 90° to the left platform. Install fences to the back of both platforms. The fences, along with the extra support of the long platforms (10 in. minimum), provide plenty of stability without having to use quick-action clamps. To keep the jig from being cut in two, leave plenty of room at the back of the base, and install a 2x4 behind the fence. The 2x4 not only adds strength but also protects your thumbs from the blade. Make sure the front of the jig is square to the table's miter groove, so you can make 90° cuts against the jig. Using the jig's base like a miter gauge saves a lot of cranking the blade over and back.

—DAVE HEFFLER, *Lakeview, N.S., Canada*

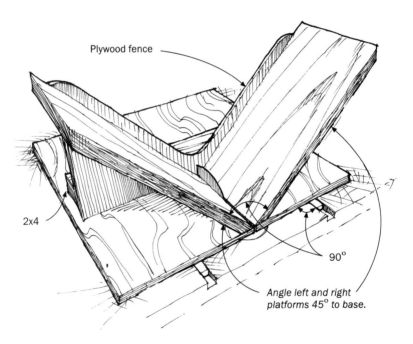

Plywood fence

2x4

90°

Angle left and right
platforms 45° to base.

Miter Fixture for Cutting Moldings

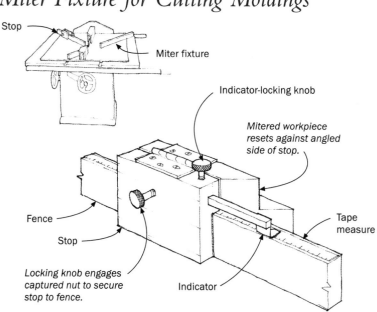

Stop

Miter fixture

Indicator-locking knob

Mitered workpiece resets against angled side of stop.

Fence

Stop

Tape measure

Locking knob engages captured nut to secure stop to fence.

Indicator

T HIS TABLESAW MITER FIXTURE has an adjustable stop to cut pic-ture frames and other moldings simply and quickly. The fixture itself is fairly standard with rails on the bottom that run in the miter-gauge slots, fences set at 45° angles and blade guards. The stop has an adjustable indicator that runs through the body of the stop. With the indicator, I can adjust the length of the cut to account for the width of the frame pieces plus clearance for the glass. Once this extra length (for any given frame material) is set into the indicator, I slide the stop along the fence and clamp when the indicator points to the actual size of the artwork. A tape measure on the fence makes it easy to read dimensions.

—JAMES R. THOMSON, *West Vancouver, B.C., Canada*

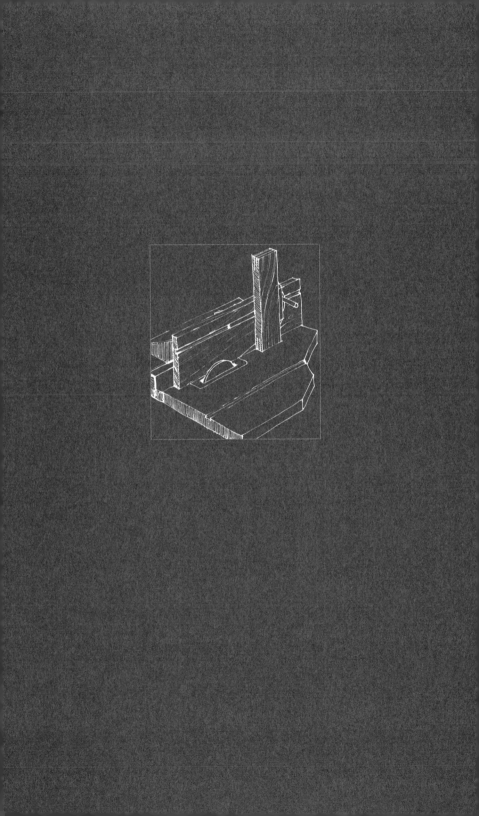

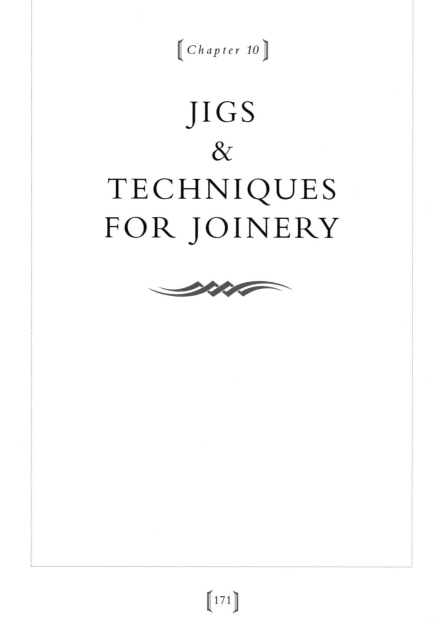

[*Chapter 10*]

JIGS
&
TECHNIQUES
FOR JOINERY

Sawing Box Joints without Tearout

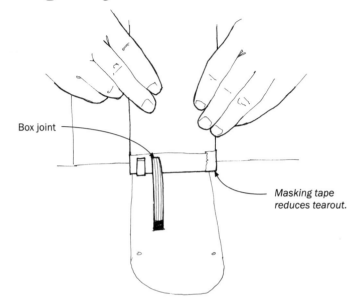

Box joint

Masking tape reduces tearout.

E VEN IF YOU HAVE A PRECISELY made jig and work carefully, tearout can be a problem when cutting box joints on a tablesaw. This is especially true with coarser-grained woods like red oak or Philippine mahogany. Fortunately, there are several good strategies for combating tearout. First, your dado set—especially the outer blades that cut the edges of each box-joint finger—must be sharp. The area on the workpiece most likely to tear out is at the back of the cut. To remedy problems here, I usually back up the workpiece with a fresh piece of ¼-in. plywood every time I make a new set of joints. Tacked to the face of the box-joint jig, the backup piece firmly supports the grain as the dado blade cuts.

The other area where tearout is common is the bottom of the cut. To avoid this, fit the tablesaw with a shopmade throat plate. This will help support grain at the end of the workpiece during cutting. First, cut a blank to fit the opening in the saw, lower the blade fully, and then start up the saw and carefully raise the blade through the new plate until it's at the depth of cut needed for your box joints.

How you handle the workpiece and jig during the cut also greatly influences the quality of the box joint. To prevent the workpiece from shifting during the cut, clamp it to the jig instead of just holding it. When making the actual cut, push the work through the blade, stop, shut off the saw and lift the jig and workpiece over the blade—never pull it backward through the running blade.

If you've done everything right and you're still having tearout problems, here are a few more tricks. Apply some masking tape over the area to be cut; drafting tape (available at stationery and drafting-supply stores) works well because it's thin and easy to remove cleanly. The tape supports the wood's surface fibers during the cut. If this fails, lightly score across the ends of the workpieces at a distance from the ends exactly equal to the depth of cut. Use a try square and a sharp knife, and score both sides as well as edges of all ends that will receive box joints.

—SANDOR NAGYSZALANCZY,
from a question by Virgil G. Klein, Wichita, Kans.

Finger-Joint Jig

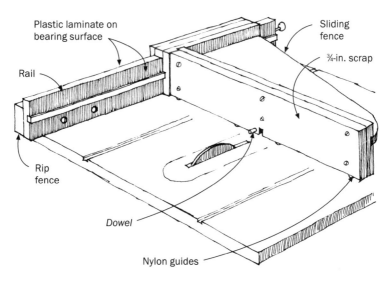

Plastic laminate on bearing surface

Sliding fence

Rail

¾-in. scrap

Rip fence

Dowel

Nylon guides

H ERE IS A FINGER-JOINT JIG that uses the tablesaw rip fence rather than the miter gauge—a sturdier, easier-to-adjust arrangement. It consists of a guide rail bolted to the saw's rip fence and a sliding-fence assembly that holds the work. Make the guide rail from particle-board or hardwood plywood and cover both sides with plastic lami-nate to reduce sliding friction. Bolt the rail to the rip fence with four ¼-in. bolts. Countersink the bolt heads on the inboard side.

As with the rail, the sliding-fence assembly is made from particle-board or plywood with plastic laminate glued to the bearing surfaces. An essential part of the jig is the hardwood tongue installed in the rail that slides in a groove in the fence assembly. Tack nylon furniture glides to the bottom of the fence assembly to allow the jig to ride freely along the table.

Set-up time is fast—a good-fitting joint can usually be achieved in two test runs. The first step is to install a dado blade for the desired finger size, say ⅜ in. Raise the dado blade about ½ in. above the thickness of the stock to be cut. Now, screw a scrap of ¾-in. material to the front of the sliding-fence assembly to serve as a disposable fence. Drill a ⅜-in. hole in the center of the scrap fence about ½ in. from the saw table. Insert a short ⅜-in. dowel in the hole to act as a guide pin. Now, adjust the rip fence/rail so that the distance between the guide pin and the dado blade is equal to the size of the dado—⅜ in. in our example.

Using a piece of scrap, start a test pass. While holding the stock vertically against the fence assembly and against the guide pin, pass the stock over the dado blade. After each cut, shift the stock to the right so that the previous cut registers over the guide pin. Start the cut in the second test piece by lining it up with the sawcut in the fence (rather than the guide pin). The joint should be snug but loose enough to allow gluing. If the joint is too tight, move the rip fence to the left. If it's too loose, move the fence to the right.

—Tom Burwell, *St. Paul, Minn.*

Making Finger Joints

THE FINGER JOINT IS NOT ONLY an effective corner joint, but it can also be used for sharp bends and curves. This method for making finger joints minimizes cumulative error. I stack up four identical 6½-in. blades on my tablesaw with spacers between them. The spacers must be made to a prescribed thickness so the slots are the same width as the fingers. First, measure the tooth width and the blade thickness with a micrometer. To calculate the spacer thickness, double the tooth width and subtract the blade thickness. The spacers can be made from items normally found around the shop, such as Formica. Wafers cut from thin sheet metal or soda cans make good fine-adjustment shims.

—KENNETH T. MAY, *Jeanerette, La.*

Perfect Half-Lap Joints

THE HALF-LAP JOINT IS A STRONG, useful joint for cabinet frames, but setting up the saw so it cuts away exactly half from each piece can be frustrating. Here's a method for setting the blade height that's fast and foolproof, and it doesn't require jigs or measuring. Grab a waste piece of the frame stock, and elevate your tablesaw's blade height to less than half the stock thickness. Pass the stock over the saw on both sides to leave a thin center section. Raise the blade a little and make a second pass. Continue raising the blade, taking cuts on both sides, until only the slightest membrane of wood remains in the center. You have now achieved the perfect blade-elevation setting. I waste the lap area with repeated passes, then clean up any small ridges and saw marks with a rasp.

—DUANE WASKOW, *Cedar Rapids, Iowa*

Plywood Edge-Banding Joint

1. Rip edging stock.   **2. Cut shoulders.**   **3. Groove plywood.**   **4. Glue and sand flush.**

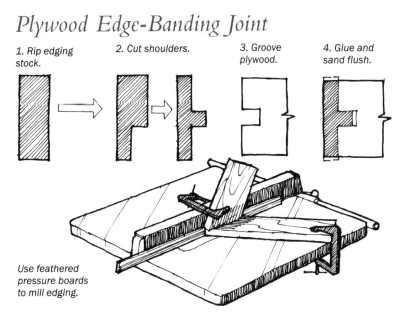

Use feathered pressure boards to mill edging.

T HIS METHOD FOR EDGING PLYWOOD is simple yet produces a very strong joint. The idea is to key the edgebanding to the plywood via a simple tongue-and-groove joint, so there is no movement when you clamp up.

First, rout a groove in the edge of the plywood using a ⅛-in. slotting cutter bit. Take care to center this groove. To make the edging, rip solid stock into thin boards, ¼ in. thick and ¹³⁄₁₆ in. wide. Using fingerboards on the tablesaw as shown in the sketch, cut a shoulder on each side of the edging to produce a tongue that fits snugly in the plywood slot. It will take you a couple of tries to get the blade set at just the right height, but once it's set you can mill 100 feet of edging very quickly. To complete, spread glue on the edging and clamp up. Later, sand down the slightly thicker lip of the banding flush with the plywood.

—V. SPIEGELMAN, *Los Angeles, Calif.*

Tablesaw Jig for Making Scarf Joints

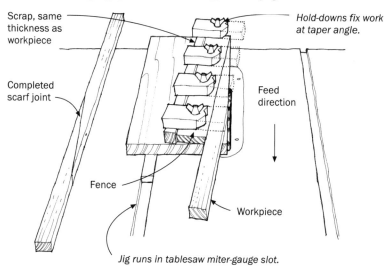

Scrap, same thickness as workpiece

Hold-downs fix work at taper angle.

Completed scarf joint

Feed direction

Fence

Workpiece

Jig runs in tablesaw miter-gauge slot.

THE SCARF JOINT, WHICH JOINS STOCK lengthwise without loss of strength, deserves more recognition outside its traditional domain of wooden boatbuilding. Here's how I make the joint for other woodworking projects.

Make a tablesaw jig from a scrap of ½-in. plywood, about 8 in. wide by 32 in. long. Attach a runner to the bottom of the jig to ride in the miter-gauge slot. Trim the edge of the jig with a pass through the sawblade. Now attach a ¾-in.-high fence angled to the blade at 5° (a slope of 12:1). Install four or five hold-downs with machine bolts and wing nuts, as shown.

To use the jig, locate the piece to be scarfed tightly against the fence, and clamp with the hold-downs. Support the left side of the hold-downs with a piece of material the same thickness as the workpiece. With the sawblade set slightly deeper than the material to be cut, make a pass through the saw.

To keep the joint parts in registration during glue up, drill a small hole through the splice, and drive in a small, round dowel or bamboo skewer.

—WILLIAM R. FULLER, *Dewitt, N.Y.*

Tenon and Bridle-Joint Jig

THIS JIG, DESIGNED TO CUT TENONS and bridle joints on the table-saw, performs as well as expensive, commercial versions.

It consists of a base, which travels in the miter-gauge slot, and a fence assembly. Dadoes in the fence assembly slide on rails in the top of the base to allow the blade-to-fence distance to be varied. The two pieces are locked at the right position by a nut mortised in a block of wood. Make the other jig parts of high-quality ¾-in. aircraft or hardwood plywood; don't waste your time with fir plywood.

To use the jig, clamp the work to the fence with a C-clamp or a hold-down clamp mounted on the fence. Align the jig for the cut, and push through the saw.

—LARRY HUMES, *Everson, Wash.*

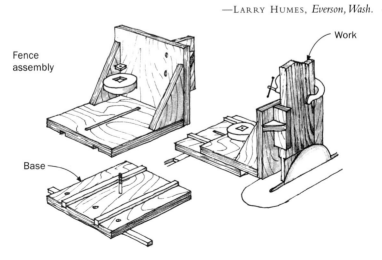

Fence assembly

Work

Base

Tablesaw Tenons with "Locked-In" Thickness

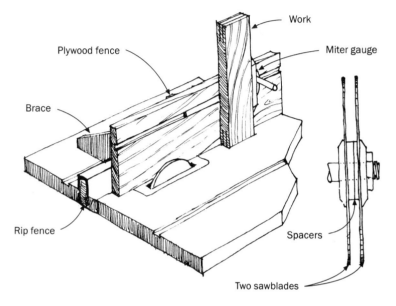

Work

Plywood fence

Miter gauge

Brace

Rip fence

Spacers

Two sawblades

T HIS METHOD FOR CUTTING TENONS on the tablesaw uses two blades with spacers between. The beauty of this system is that the tenon thickness is "locked in" and does not depend on variables such as stock thickness or pressure against the fence.

I keep a pair of special hollow-ground blades for tenon work. They are jointed as a pair and filed for ripping. Since the hub and tooth thickness are the same, cutting a ⅝₆-in. tenon, for example, simply requires mounting the two blades with a ¼-in. and a ¹⁄₁₆-in. spacer between. My set of custom-machined spacers consists of 2½-in. disks drilled to slip over the saw arbor. Spacer thicknesses range from ¼ in. to 0.005 in. To pass the work through the blades, I use a standard miter gauge tracked in a plywood fence as shown above. This approach eliminates vertical rocking and thus is safer and more accurate than other methods.

—MAC CAMPBELL, *Harvey Station, N.B., Canada*

Tablesaw Tenoning Jig

FACED WITH CUTTING 32 TENONS on a recent project, I priced a new Delta tenoning jig and found it beyond my budget. So I put myself to work and made the jig pictured here at the cost of a few ¾-in. plywood scraps and some hardware items already in my shop. It consists of a baseplate that rides along the miter-gauge slot and a top table that adjusts closer to or farther from the sawblade. The work is clamped both against the jig's face and a vertical stop block, which can be pivoted to an angle if necessary.

To cut the tenons, I installed two identical 8-in. blades on my saw arbor with a ½-in. spacer between. I had the 32 tenons cut in no time.

—HARRIE E. BURNELL, *Newburyport, Mass.*

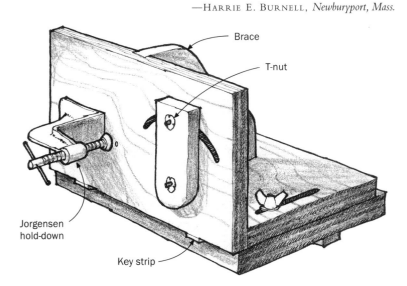

Brace

T-nut

Jorgensen
hold-down

Key strip

Tablesaw Tenoning Fixture

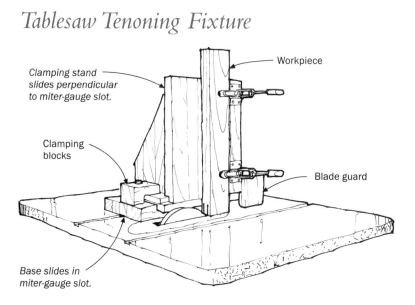

Clamping stand slides perpendicular to miter-gauge slot.

Workpiece

Clamping blocks

Blade guard

Base slides in miter-gauge slot.

A GOOD TENONING FIXTURE for a tablesaw must be heavy, strong, rigid and accurate. That's why I made my massive tenoning fixture from an old laminated maple, science-lab tabletop. The fixture has two main parts: a base that slides in the miter-gauge slot on a steel key and a vertical clamping stand that slides across the base perpendicular to the miter-gauge slot. Clamping blocks are bolted into the base to hold the vertical stand in place after it's been moved into position to cut the correct-size tenon. Permanently attached lever-action clamps, like those by De-Sta-Co., are screwed to the fence on the vertical stand to hold the workpiece. As a safety feature, I added a blade guard on the trailing end of the fixture.

On production runs, I cut the tenon in one pass by mounting two identical blades separated by spacers, which set the final thickness of the tenon. Normally, though, when I have just one or two tenons to cut, I use a single blade and flip the workpiece for the second cut.

—JOE MOORE, *Brockville, Ont., Canada*

Adjustable Stop for Cutting Tenons

HERE IS A SIMPLE STOP-FIXTURE that I use to cut perfect tenon shoulders. The device, which is attached to my cutoff jig, prevents tenon-cheek waste from jamming against the fence, as often happens when using the rip fence as a stop. I just cut the workpiece to the right length, and the stop does the rest.

—JOHN W. WILLIAMS, *Bellevue, Wash.*

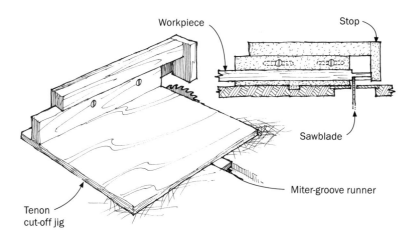

Workpiece

Stop

Sawblade

Miter-groove runner

Tenon
cut-off jig

Stationary Jig for Cutting Open Mortises

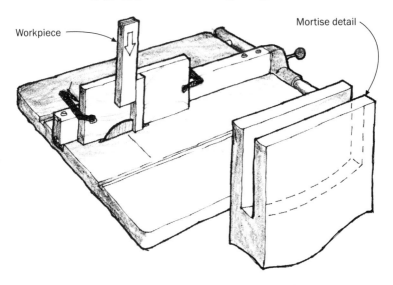

Workpiece

Mortise detail

T HE JIG SHOWN ABOVE IS USED to cut open bridle-joint mortises in frame members. It solves many of the problems inherent with sliding jigs, which tend to be complicated to make and adjust and which sometimes wobble during the cut. The only disadvantage is that the jig leaves a slight concavity at the bottom of the mortise, as shown in the drawing. This space doesn't show in the finished joint, however, and since it's end grain, the missing wood isn't critical to joint strength.

Make the jig by screwing a hardwood fence to an 8-in.-wide piece of ¾-in. plywood. Clamp the jig to the rip fence so that the frame member to be mortised will be centered over the saw arbor. Adjust the rip fence so that the sawblade is the proper cheek thickness from the jig.

To cut the mortise, hold the workpiece firmly against the plywood, with its back edge tight to the hardwood fence. Plunge the work down the fence onto the blade. Draw it up, flip it and cut the other cheek. On narrow stock, this will complete the mortise. For wider stock, chisel out the waste.

—FREDERICK J. MILLER, *Chatsworth, Ont., Canada*

Cutting Angled Tenons on the Tablesaw

WHEN CUTTING ANGLED TENONS like the kind needed on aprons of tapered-leg tables, using your tablesaw's miter gauge can be prone to error. And setting the miter gauge to the exact but opposite angle to cut the other side of the tenon is time-consuming. An easy solution exists. Cut your desired angle in a long piece of scrap, and then insert the scrap to add or subtract this angle from your normal 90° setup. If the miter gauge's 90° fence is accurate, the opposites will match exactly. Add a strip of sandpaper to the contact surfaces of the scrap to prevent slippage.

—ROBERT J. CLARK, *Holland, Mich.*

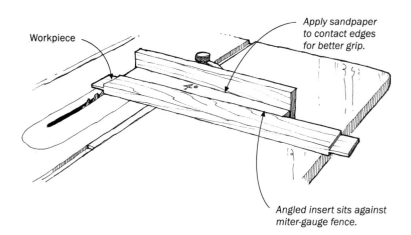

Workpiece

Apply sandpaper to contact edges for better grip.

Angled insert sits against miter-gauge fence.

Cutting Corner Bridle Joints

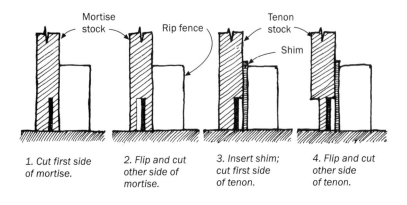

| 1. Cut first side of mortise. | 2. Flip and cut other side of mortise. | 3. Insert shim; cut first side of tenon. | 4. Flip and cut other side of tenon. |

THIS PROCEDURE ELIMINATES THE TEDIOUS fence adjustments and frustrating ⅟₃₂-in. errors that go with cutting open mortise-and-tenon joints on the tablesaw. It is based on a thin auxiliary fence or shim that's exactly as thick as the saw kerf of the blade you're using. The shim stock, made of thin plywood (door skin) or surfaced from solid stock, should be as wide as your fence is tall and should be long enough to clamp to your fence—say, 8 in. by 16 in.

To use, set up the saw to cut the open mortise. Saw the mortise as usual by passing both cheeks of the stock over the blade. Do not adjust the fence to saw the tenon. Simply clamp the shim to the fence and saw out the tenon—first one face, then the other. The shim repositions the tenon stock just to the other side of the cut line. The joint will be just right.

—JOHN F. ANDERSON, *Bottineau, N.D.,*
and Ivan Hentschel, Kingston, N.J.

Consistent Dadoes on the Tablesaw

THE SECRET OF THIS SIMPLE WOODEN TABLESAW insert is the hump in the middle. Because the work will touch only at the high point of the hump, dadoes and grooves will be consistently the same depth regardless of slight waves and warps in the wood.

—DAVID WARD, *Loveland, Colo.*

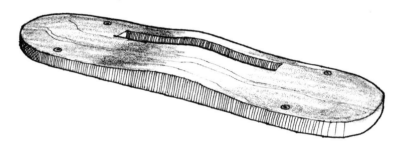

Enlarging a Dado with Tape

WHEN YOU NEED TO ENLARGE A TABLESAW DADO by just a hair, tape a piece of paper to the fence, and run the piece through again. Papers of different thicknesses will vary the adjustment in the dado. The results are much more accurate than trying to move the fence.

—JACK KEGLEY, *Charlottesville, Va.*

Spacing Dadoes

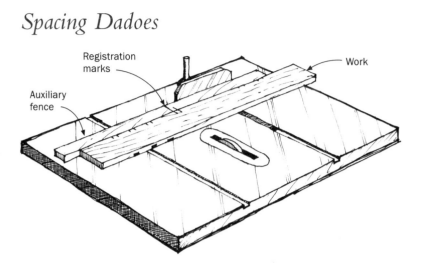

Registration marks

Work

Auxiliary fence

R ECENTLY, WHILE BUILDING A CABINET for cassette tapes, I experimented with several methods for spacing the numerous dadoes needed. Using an auxiliary miter-gauge fence gave the measure of accuracy and easy use I sought.

Bolt a piece of wood the length of the saw table and about 1 in. wide to the miter gauge. This auxiliary fence becomes an extension of the gauge, stabilizing long pieces of work and preventing twisting on the saw. The auxiliary fence should be the same thickness as the workpiece. After the dado width is set and tested on scrap, make a cut into the auxiliary fence. Mark the right and left edges of the cut on the top of the fence. The workpiece, marked for spacing, is moved along the auxiliary fence. When the lines meet, slide the gauge into the dado blade, making the cut.

—PAUL SAFFRON, *Rockville Centre, N.Y.*

EDITOR'S NOTE: A variation of Saffron's method is common practice in many cabinet shops. Screw a new auxiliary fence to the miter gauge and trim off the excess by pushing the fence through the saw. Since the end of the fence now coincides exactly with the saw kerf, it can be used for accurate cutoff work. Just slide the mark on the workpiece up to the end of the fence, and push through the saw.

Cut Twice for Better Square Cuts

MOST TABLESAW AND RADIAL-ARM SAWBLADES that I've worked with have a tendency to climb and squirm when crosscutting. The result is an out-of-square cut. I've found, quite by accident, that if the crosscut is very thin, say one half the kerf, the saw cuts amazingly true. This approach does require that you make two cuts—one to rough length (leaving a half-kerf extra) and the second to final length. Of course, if the machine is out of square to begin with, all bets are off.

—PAT WARNER, *Escondido, Calif.*

Tablesaw Rabbet/Dado Jig

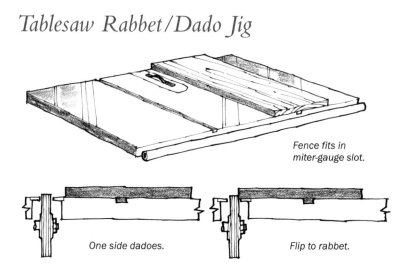

Fence fits in
miter-gauge slot.

One side dadoes.

Flip to rabbet.

B ECAUSE THE PLYWOOD END PANELS I make for kitchen cabinet
jobs are usually worked the same way each time, I found myself
setting the rip fence to the same measurements for dadoes and rabbets
time and time again. The simple fixture above solved this problem
because it is essentially a premeasured rip fence that I can use instantly
by just popping it into the miter-gauge slot. It's a dual-purpose fixture:
I just lift it out of the slot, turn it end for end and push it back down
into the slot to use the other side. One side cuts dadoes 2 in. from the
edge of the workpiece; the other side cuts ¾-in. rabbets.

The rabbet/dado fixture worked so well that I made a second
variation strictly for rabbeting. One edge is sized to cut ⅜-in. rabbets
and the other to cut ¼-in. rabbets. I discovered on this second jig that
it's best to make the fixture to mount in the right-hand miter-gauge
slot if your sawblade slides on the arbor from the right (and vice versa
if your blade slides on from the left). If made this way, the fixture can
be used with virtually any-width dado head.

—DON RUSSELL, *Auburn, Calif.*

Dado Spacers from old PC Hard Drives

O LD HARD DRIVES FROM PERSONAL COMPUTERS contain several useful components. The bearings and spindle make a smooth-working lazy Susan, and the platters make excellent ½-in.-thick spacers for a tablesaw dado blade.

—JIM CLIFTON, *Kalamazoo, Mich.*

Straightening Curved Lumber

H ERE'S A TRICK FOR STRAIGHTENING a bowed board. Tape a piece of angle iron to the concave edge of the board to serve as a guide, as shown below. If the board is thin, block up the angle iron so it won't drag on the table. Pass the board through the saw with the flat edge of the angle iron against the rip fence. Remove the iron, flip the board and pass through the saw again. The result is a straight board with parallel sides.

—CHARLES F. RIORDAN, *Dansville, N.Y.*

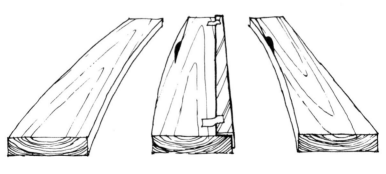

Bowed board

Tape angle iron to concave edge; rip to true one edge.

Flip and rip to true other edge.

Making Dadoes with a Dog Board

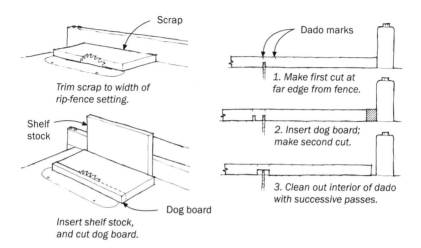

Trim scrap to width of
rip-fence setting.

Shelf
stock

Dog board

Insert shelf stock,
and cut dog board.

Dado marks

1. Make first cut at
far edge from fence.

2. Insert dog board;
make second cut.

3. Clean out interior of dado
with successive passes.

I DEVISED THIS METHOD so that I could cut a few dadoes quickly and accurately without having to adjust a set of dado cutters to an exact width with paper shims. The key to this method is a strip of scrap, which I call a dog board, that shifts the workpiece the exact distance needed to cut both sides of the dado.

To make the dog board, trim a piece of scrap to a random width. Insert a piece of the shelf stock between the scrap and the fence. Run the scrap through the saw, and save the cutoff. You now have the dog board.

To use the dog board, mark the dado locations on the workpiece, and set the rip fence and blade height for the first cut, the one farthest from the rip fence. Make the cut. Now, insert the dog board between the workpiece and the fence, and make the second cut. Nibble out the waste between the two cuts with successive passes. The dado will fit the shelf stock perfectly.

—JAMES KIMBRIEL, *Batavia, N.Y.*

Tablesaw Jointing Fixture

I WOULDN'T TRY THIS SETUP on a board shorter than 10 ft., but one of the handiest jigs in my shop is a tablesaw setup for straightening the edges of 1-in. hardwood boards. It does the same job as the jointer, but it is faster and more convenient for the 18-ft. boards I use in my boat shop.

To build the jig, joint a 7-ft. long 1x2, and cut a long tapering point on one end. Glue the 1x2 to a ¾-in. plywood base, about 8 ft. long. Cut a slot in the base in front of the fence for the tablesaw blade.

To use, clamp the fixture to the saw table with the 1x2 fence flush with the left-hand face of the sawblade at its rear edge. Support the tail of the fixture so that it's level. As you pass a board over the sawblade, the waste edge is split away by the long bevel. Press the board tight to the 1x2 fence to get a straight edge.

You do have to freehand the first 6 in. or 7 in. of the cut, as the board must pass the sawblade before it picks up the fence. Freehand cuts can easily kick back, so be careful.

—COLIN PITTENDRIGH, *Bozeman, Mont.*

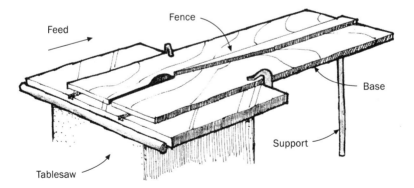

Jointing on the Tablesaw

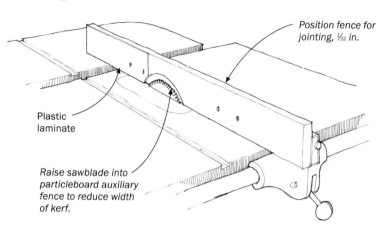

Position fence for
jointing, ½₂ in.

Plastic
laminate

Raise sawblade into
particleboard auxiliary
fence to reduce width
of kerf.

I NEEDED TO JOINT THE EDGE of a 1½-in.-thick tabletop laminated
up from two pieces of ¾-in. particleboard. The piece was too long
and unwieldy for my jointer, and I didn't want to dull my knives on
the particleboard. So I used this technique to joint the workpiece on
the tablesaw.

Make an auxiliary fence the same height as your saw's rip fence.
Contact-cement a strip of ½₂-in.-thick plastic laminate to the face of
the auxiliary fence. Screw the auxiliary fence to the rip fence, lower
the blade and adjust the fence location until the plastic laminate is
flush with the edge of the blade. Turn on the saw, and slowly raise the
blade, cutting a kerf into the auxiliary fence.

Place the piece to be jointed flat on the saw table, hold the workpiece against the fence and push it through the blade. The far end of
the fence will act as an outfeed table. Each pass will remove about
½₂ in. of material, the same thickness as the laminate.

—GARY P. WESTMORELAND, *Apple Valley, Calif.*

Setting a Tablesaw Blade at 90°

THE TIME-HONORED WAY FOR SETTING a tablesaw blade so that it cuts a true 90° angle is to raise it up to its full height and put a square against it, carefully avoiding any of the teeth. I used this method for many years but never found it completely satisfactory for two reasons. If you have a wobbling blade or a throat insert that isn't level, you don't get an accurate reading.

I now use another technique that's easy to set up and totally accurate. Select a piece of 2x8 scrap a foot or so in length, and plane both sides of it. Trim both edges of the block with the blade fully raised. Remove the sawdust from the saw table, and stand the block on one of the freshly trimmed edges. Place a try square against the block. A board this wide and this thick will give a highly accurate reading against a good square. Adjust the tilt of the blade, and trim the block again, until the cut is perfectly square.

—THOMAS J. BROOKS JR., *Jackson, Miss.*

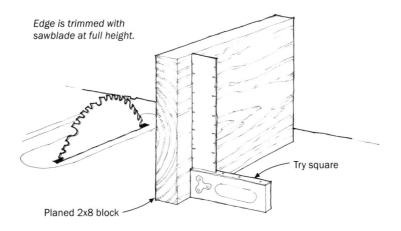

Edge is trimmed with sawblade at full height.

Try square

Planed 2x8 block

A Jig to Set Accurate Saw Angles

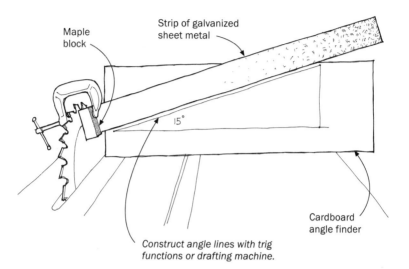

Maple block

Strip of galvanized sheet metal

15°

Cardboard angle finder

Construct angle lines with trig functions or drafting machine.

WHEN I WANTED TO MAKE A SEGMENTED cylinder on my table-saw, I discovered the importance of setting the blade at the exact tilt angle. But the tilt scales provided on the saw are imprecise at best. So I developed this technique that—if carefully done—will produce a blade-tilt angle accurate to within one one-hundredth of a degree.

The key to this technique is a flat, parallel strip of 22-gauge, galvanized sheet metal, about 1 in. or so wide and 10 in. long. Add epoxy, and screw the strip to a ½-in.-sq., 1-in.-long block of hard maple. The accuracy of the final sawblade setting is directly proportional to how square the wood block is to the edge of the metal strip, so take care when fastening them together.

To use this device, crank up the blade part way, and then clamp it onto the blade with a small C-clamp. Be sure to clamp the wooden part to a flat, clean area of the blade, avoiding any carbide teeth that are thicker. The metal strip serves as an indicator: The angle at which it is inclined is an accurate gauge of the tilt angle of the blade.

For each desired angle setting, make up an angle finder from a piece of cardboard. Scribe the desired angle on the cardboard using a drafting machine, or construct the angle using trigonometric functions and a calculator. Place the cardboard finder behind the gauge, and then tilt the blade until the angle matches the line on the finder.

—HELMUT WOLF, *Albuquerque, N.M.*

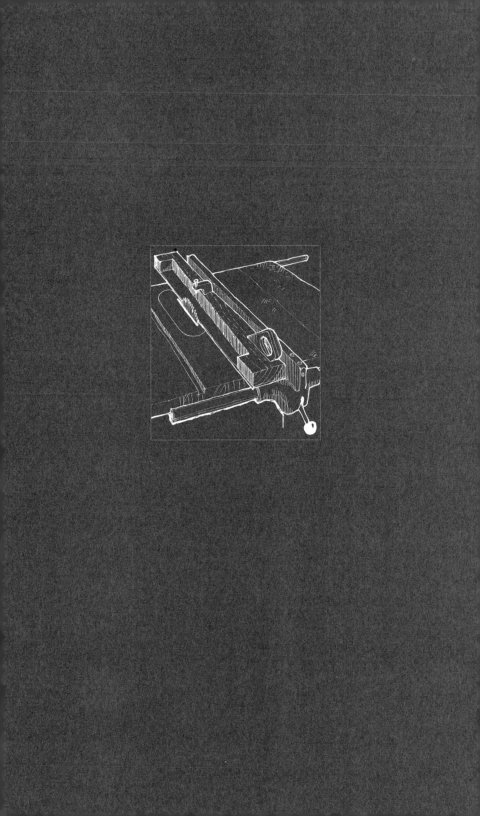

FLUTING,
COVING
&
TAPERING JIGS

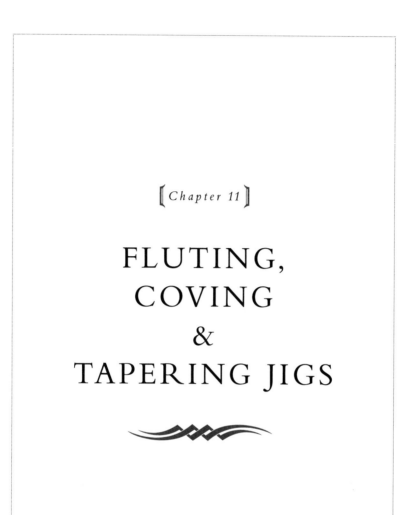

Cove Molding on the Tablesaw

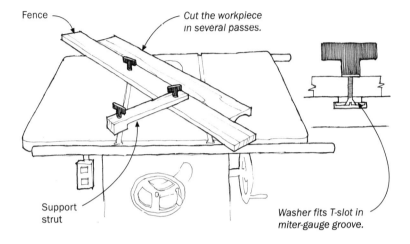

Fence

Cut the workpiece in several passes.

Support strut

Washer fits T-slot in miter-gauge groove.

I F YOU CUT A LOT OF COVE MOLDING on your tablesaw, this fixture will quickly repay the time invested in making it. The fixture requires a T-shaped miter-gauge slot, which is found on most tablesaws. To make the fixture, start by selecting a flat washer that fits the T-slot. Countersink two washers to fit the head of a machine screw. The washers and screws will provide hold-downs for adjusting and locking the fence in place. Select a clear, straight 1¼-in.-thick board for the fence. Assemble the fence and the support strut with the hold-downs and knobs, as shown in the sketch. You can buy the knobs or make your own.

To adjust the fence, set the sawblade at the full height of the finish cut. Move the fence to the near side of the blade. With a second straightedge held just tangent to the far side of the blade and parallel to the fence, vary the angle of the fence until you get the correct width of the cove between the fence and the straightedge. Tighten the knobs to lock the fence in place, lower the blade until about ⅟₁₆ in.

protrudes above the table surface, and make the first pass to produce a small concave cut. Make successive cuts raising the blade ⅟₁₆ in. on each pass until you reach the desired cove depth.

—ROY H. HOFFMAN, *Oriental, N.C.*

Tablesawn Coves with a Molding Head

I'VE SEEN SEVERAL ARTICLES LATELY describing how to cut coves by pushing the workpiece across the tablesaw at an angle using temporary guide fences. The trouble is they're all doing it the same way it was done 50 years ago—scratching rough coves ⅟₁₆ in. at a time with sawblades that were designed to cut kerfs.

To cut smooth coves to full depth in one pass, simply replace the sawblade with a molding head fitted with radiused cutters. The molding head removes fluffy shavings—evidence that it is cutting, as opposed to whatever a sawblade does when the work is fed into it from the side. A second cut of ⅟₃₂ in. will produce a finish comparable to that of a commercially milled molding. Of course, for a very deep cove, you can remove the waste in more than one pass.

Cove cutting is not for unsupervised beginners. Beyond the generally accepted safe work habits, I recommend a few special measures. First, use a snug-fitting insert, making sure it is flush to the saw's surface. Make sure the angled fence is held securely in place, and the cutters are sharp and clean. Apply wax to both table and guides so that the work will slide easily. Do not use push sticks; push blocks are much better for this operation. You can make your own push blocks from the rubber-padded floats used for finishing concrete. Last of all, feed the stock at a slow, steady rate. You will be delighted with the results.

—TOM ROSE, *Los Angeles, Calif.*

Angle Finder for Cutting Coves

Set parallelogram jig to desired cove width; place
jig astride blade to determine fence angle.

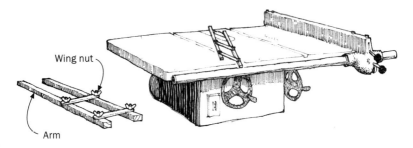

Wing nut

Arm

To accurately cut coves on the tablesaw, you must clamp
the fence to the table at the correct angle, because the angle
determines the shape of the cove. This simple parallelogram device
makes finding the correct fence angle easy.

To use the device, simply move the arms apart a distance equal to
the desired width of the cove, and tighten the wing nuts to lock the
arms. With the sawblade set as high as the cove will be deep, place the
device over the blade and rotate it until the arms contact the tips of
the teeth at front and back. The device is now at the correct fence
angle. All that remains is to clamp a fence to the saw at the same angle
and, taking about ⅛ in. at a pass, begin making incremental cove cuts
until the final depth is reached.

—Joe Hardy, *Des Moines, Iowa*

Ogee Molding

OGEE MOLDING IS EASY TO MAKE using the tablesaw along with a jointer or handplane. By setting up a diagonal fence on the tablesaw, the boards —usually 3 in. to 5 in. wide—are hollowed, leaving a flat section along each edge, one narrow and one wider. For 4-in. molding of the type usually used for bracket feet on case pieces, I usually leave a ¾-in. flat along one edge, which will remain flat. Along the other edge is a wider plane, which I joint or handplane into the graceful curve that makes this molding so useful. For safety, always use a push stick, and make several passes over the tablesaw blade, raising it perhaps ⅛ in. at each pass. The fence is simply a board with a straight edge, clamped to the saw table at about 30° to the line of the blade. Other moldings, chair seats and even raised panels with beautiful curves forming the rise may be made using variations of this method.

—JAMES B. SMALL, JR., *Newville, Pa.*

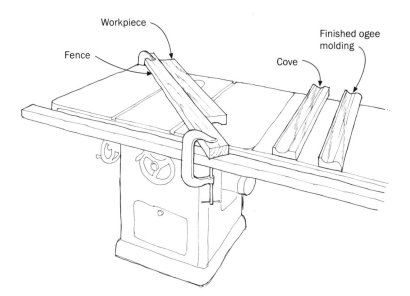

Fence

Workpiece

Finished ogee molding

Cove

Making Fluted Panels on the Tablesaw

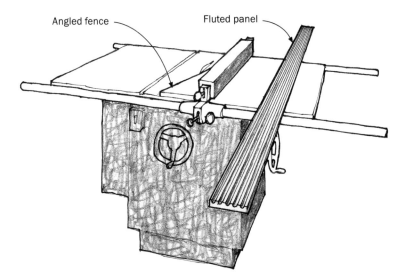

Angled fence

Fluted panel

WHEN I NEEDED TWO 7-FT.-LONG FLUTED panels for the front entrance of my house, I made this simple angled fence and cut the flutes on my tablesaw. The fence is simply a wedge-shaped piece of plywood screwed to a plywood channel that press-fits on the rip fence. The angle of the plywood to the blade will determine the shape of the flutes, with a small angle producing deep, narrow flutes and a larger angle producing shallow, wide flutes. I found that an angle of 13° was about right for this particular job.

To cut the fluted panels, fix the angled fence on the rip fence and set the blade depth at about ⅛ in. It will take four passes, raising the blade ⅛ in. after each pass, to cut the flute to its final depth of ½ in. After one flute has been completed, move the rip fence over, lower the blade and start another.

—WAYNE A. KULESZA, *Chicago, Ill.*

Making Fluted Panels Revisited

H ERE'S AN IMPROVEMENT TO WAYNE KULESZA'S method (on the facing page) for making fluted panels. First, determine the proper fence angle to produce the flute width desired, then clamp an auxiliary fence to the saw. Tape several spacer strips to the side of the workpiece; the width of the spacer strips determines the distance between flutes. Push the workpiece and spacers through the saw to cut the first flute. If your blade is sharp and the flute not too deep, it should be possible to cut each flute in one pass. After you have sawn the first flute, slice off the outermost spacer by cutting the tape with a utility knife. Continue making passes and removing spacers until you have completed the panel. The spacer strips eliminate the time required in resetting the fence for each pass through the blade.

If the blade binds and prevents you from cutting each flute in one pass, there are two alternatives. You can raise the blade in increments as you cut each flute. Or you can make a series of shallow flutes across the width of the board, then replace the spacer strips, raise the blade and repeat the series until full depth is achieved. To ensure equal depth on all flutes, I would choose the second alternative.

—JOE VIDETIC, *Joliet, Ill.*

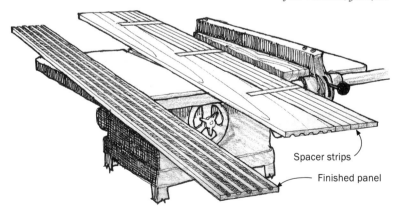

Spacer strips

Finished panel

Making a Safer Taper Jig

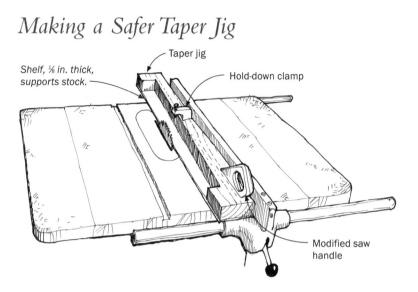

Taper jig

Shelf, ⅛ in. thick,
supports stock.

Hold-down clamp

Modified saw
handle

Y OU CAN MAKE A SHOP-BUILT TABLESAW taper jig safer and easier
to use by adding a ⅛-in.-thick plywood or Masonite shelf to the
bottom and a hold-down clamp and a handle to the top. The shelf-
and-hold-down combination holds the workpiece snugly enough to
eliminate the balancing act that usually accompanies cutting tapers.
The combination also lets you push the jig through as a unit with
your hand far away from the blade. I find that the system is especially
good for tapering narrow table legs.

—JOE VOLTAS, *Fall River, Mass.*

One-Minute Taper Jig

I USE A JIG TO TAPER A GUITAR'S FINGERBOARDS, but the jig could be adapted to table legs or any short tapering job. The limiting factor is the length of the rip fence.

Start with a piece of hardwood scrap that's narrower than the work. Cut a notch into both ends of the scrap to leave two fingers. One finger should be half as wide as the taper, and the other finger should be as wide as the taper. To use the jig, first rip the workpiece. Then, without changing the fence setting, insert the half-taper notch between the fence and the workpiece, and trim one side. Flip the workpiece over and flip the jig end for end to trim the second side. The resulting workpiece will have square ends and equal tapers.

—PHIL CLARK, *Homestead, Pa.*

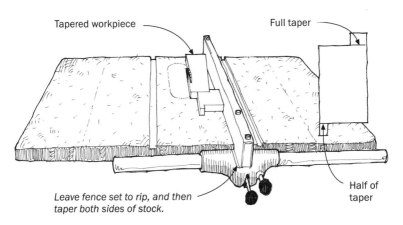

Tapered workpiece

Full taper

Leave fence set to rip, and then taper both sides of stock.

Half of taper

Improved Taper Jig

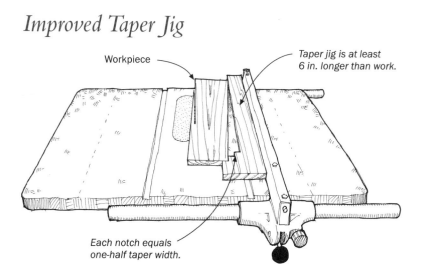

Workpiece

Taper jig is at least
6 in. longer than work.

Each notch equals
one-half taper width.

T HE TAPERING JIG I USE FOR SHORT runs is just as quick to make
as Phil Clark's (described in the previous tip), but it also handles
longer workpieces and provides more control and safety. I simply cut
three notches into a scrap piece that's 6 in. or so longer than the
workpiece to be tapered. The width of each notch is one-half the
taper. For longer runs or if the final taper is too small to hold securely
and safely, I attach the jig to a substrate and use De-Sta-Co toggle
clamps to hold the workpiece firmly.

—TAI LAKE, *Holualoa, Hawaii*

Quick Tapers on the Tablesaw

HERE'S A QUICK AND FOOLPROOF WAY to cut tapers. First, draw the desired cut line on the workpiece in pencil. Set the saw fence to a width slightly greater than the workpiece, and cut a scrap of hardboard to this width. Using either double-faced tape or tacks, affix the hardboard to the workpiece, carefully aligning the edge of the hardboard to the pencil line. Run this assembly through the saw without resetting the fence.

The saw will cut a precise taper, right to the line.

—LEIGH JERRARD, *Los Angeles, Calif.*

Attach hardboard to workpiece, lining
up the edge to the marked line.

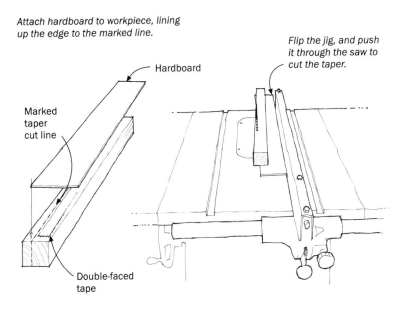

Flip the jig, and push
it through the saw to
cut the taper.

Hardboard

Marked
taper
cut line

Double-faced
tape

Tapering Jig Can Handle Small Pieces

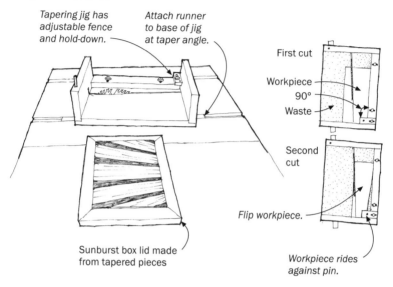

Tapering jig has adjustable fence and hold-down.

Attach runner to base of jig at taper angle.

First cut

Workpiece

90°

Waste

Second cut

Flip workpiece.

Sunburst box lid made from tapered pieces

Workpiece rides against pin.

M Y JEWELRY BOXES FEATURE a sunburst pattern on the lid, which I make by gluing up nine or so tapered pieces into a fan shape. The jig that I use to cut these small tapered workpieces on my tablesaw is built like a miniature sliding crosscut table. One big difference, however, is that the runner (which fits in the tablesaw's miter-gauge slot) is attached at an angle to the centerline of the jig. The runner angle should be half the desired taper angle, which for my jig is 4°. An adjustable fence to the right of the kerf determines the width of the tapered piece's wider end. The lower end of this fence has an adjustable hold-down that registers the workpiece for the second pass. With this jig, you can vary the width of the workpiece but not the taper angle.

To equally taper both edges of the work, I draw each tapered piece to scale, and then I measure the dimensions. Next, I set the jig's fence to the width of the workpiece's wider end (the end that meets the sawblade first), and I make the first taper cut. I place a brass pin (stored in the jig's rear cross brace when not in use) in the hold-down and adjust the pin to the width of the trapezoid's narrower end. I then flip the blank over and make the second cut.

—DAVID M. FREEDMAN, *Cross Plains, Wisc.*

A Jig for Small Tapers

TAPERING SMALL PIECES OF WOOD, say 7 in. long or so, on the tablesaw with a traditional tapering jig can be scary and outright dangerous. You have to hold the small piece with just your fingertip near the blade. Beads of sweat should break out on your brow as you consider doing this.

My first suggestion for tapering small workpieces is to do it on the bandsaw with a fine 6-teeth-per-inch (tpi) blade or one of the Wood Slicer blades that Highland Hardware carries. The tip of a pencil will hold your work in a taper jig that runs against a bandsaw fence. You can use the standard taper jig with an infinitely adjustable angling fence or make a dedicated jig out of a piece of plywood. And because all of the blade's force is downward on a bandsaw, it will make your work much safer.

Another method is to make a tapering jig with a hold-down built into it. You can then use this jig on either the tablesaw or the router. Use a plate of ¼-in. material, such as plywood, medium-density fiberboard (MDF) or Masonite, and mount a fence with a stop on it. This fence will be either adjustable or set at the appropriate angle to yield the taper you want (for example, a ⅜-in. taper over 7 in.). Then on top of the fence or just behind it, mount a quick-action De-Sta-Co clamp that will hold the workpiece flat to the ¼-in. plate. You then pass this whole setup past the blade or bit. Keep your fingers on top of the clamp so they're away from the bit and out of danger. For ease and safety, be sure to make this jig longer and wider than what you need. On the router table, be sure you feed into the rotation of the bit, so it does not take your piece and throw it rudely across the shop. And if you have lots of tapers to make, check the jig every so often to make sure the jig is still accurate and you're safe.

—GARY ROGOWSKI,
from a question by M. Zazvorkia, Burnbury, B.C., Canada

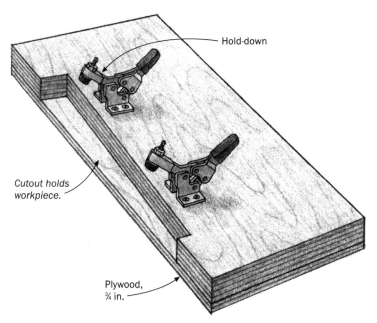

Hold-down

Cutout holds
workpiece.

Plywood,
¾ in.

Jig for Cutting Wedges

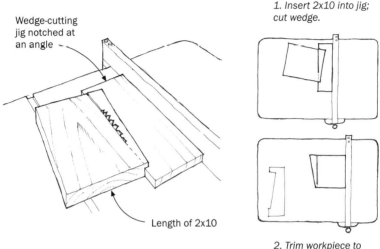

Wedge-cutting
jig notched at
an angle

Length of 2x10

1. Insert 2x10 into jig;
cut wedge.

2. Trim workpiece to
make second wedge.

I JUST GLUED UP THREE LARGE CHERRY PANELS using a vertical press
that relies on a lot of wedges to work. Here's how I cut the wedges
quickly and accurately with a simple jig.

Start by notching a scrap of plywood with the desired wedge shape,
as shown in the sketch. Cut a short length from a 2x10 to fit the
notch in the plywood snugly. Place the workpiece into the notch, and
run the plywood against the fence to slice off a wedge. Remove the
wedge from the jig, and run the uncut edge of the 2x10 against the
fence to produce a second wedge. Continue this sequence of cuts until
the 2x10 is too small to handle safely.

—KARL KIRCHHOFER, Seattle, Wash.

Cutting Stretchers for Tapered Legs

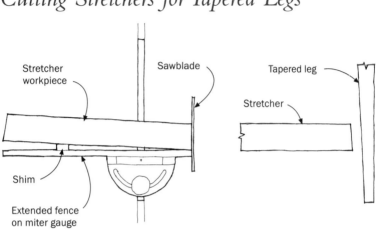

Stretcher workpiece

Sawblade

Tapered leg

Stretcher

Shim

Extended fence on miter gauge

T HE ENDS OF STRETCHERS THAT JOIN to tapered table legs must be crosscut at the same angle to join the legs properly. You can calculate the angle and set the tablesaw miter gauge to the calculated angle. But there is an easier and more accurate method—similar to the way carpenters cut roof rafters.

Characterize the taper as x in. of taper over y in. of length. When you consider the taper in this way, it's easy to set the proper angle by leaving the miter gauge set at 90° and shimming the stretcher out from the miter gauge to get the correct angle.

For example, if the leg tapers ¼ in. over each 12 in. of length, place a ¼-in. shim 12 in. from the sawblade to set the correct angle of the stretcher cut. Cut one end of the stretcher; then flip it over, and cut the other end to the desired length. If necessary, you can use a smaller shim closer to the blade if you maintain the same x to y ratio. In the example cited, a ⅛-in. shim 6 in. from the blade would accomplish the same result.

—JAMES POTZICK, *Potomac, Md.*

Cutting Tapered Wedges on the Tablesaw

I LIKE TO USE THE WEDGED THROUGH-TENON JOINT and have developed a way to cut consistently tapered wedges quickly on the tablesaw. The key to the method is to save the waste cutoff ends of glued-up tabletops and the like. I use a tablesaw jig to taper one edge of these scraps at ½ in. per foot, or 2° (the taper shown in the sketch is exaggerated to about 5° for clarity). To cut wedges, I simply crosscut the tapered scrap piece, flipping the piece after each cut. Rather than measure, I eyeball the width of the wedge, making sure to cut the thin end of the wedge smaller than needed. When fitting the wedge, I trim off the thin end with tin snips until the wedge fits the kerf in the tenon perfectly.

—C. M. CHAPPELL, *Houston, Tex.*

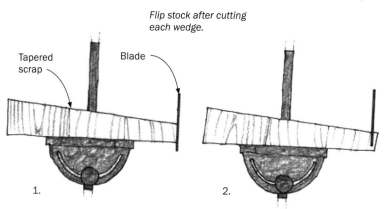

Flip stock after cutting
each wedge.

Tapered
scrap

Blade

1.

2.

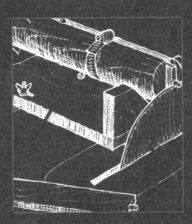

[*Chapter 12*]

RAISING
PANELS
&
SHAPING

Rip-Fence-Straddling Jig for Fielded Panels

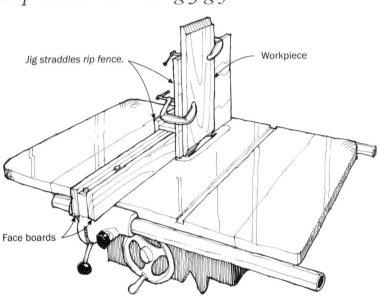

Jig straddles rip fence.

Workpiece

Face boards

T HIS JIG IS DESIGNED SPECIFICALLY for making those steep angled cuts on the edges of long workpieces, as in making fielded panel doors. If you've tried sliding a wobbling workpiece vertically along the fence, while watching to make sure the tapered end doesn't fall through the space in the saw insert, you'll immediately recognize the advantages of this jig. With it, you can make a smooth, controlled, burn-free cut.

Dimensions aren't critical; just make sure the jig slides smoothly on the rip fence. The face of the jig can be large or small depending on the size of the workpiece. It can be fitted with a vertical fence if needed. Just C-clamp the workpiece to the face of the jig, then slide the jig past the blade.

—ALFRED W. SWETT, *Portland, Maine*

Panel-Raising Fixture

I MADE THIS FIXTURE TO EXPEDITE making dozens of ½-in.-thick red oak panels 1 ft. wide by 5 ft. tall. The height of the sawblade and the slope of the fixture produces panels beveled at 7½°, with the shoulder of the field cut simultaneously. If you push the panels through carefully and use a high-quality carbide blade, you'll produce panels that are virtually free of machine marks and require minimal sanding.

—WARREN W. BENDER JR., *Medford, N.Y.*

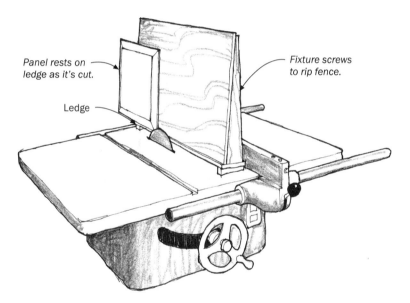

Panel rests on ledge as it's cut.

Fixture screws to rip fence.

Ledge

Raising Arched Panels

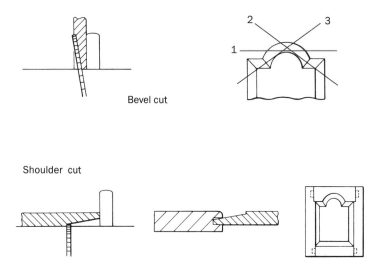

Bevel cut

Shoulder cut

T HE SHAPER IS THE CORRECT TOOL for making a raised panel door with an arched top. I don't have a shaper, so I do the job the hard way, with the tablesaw and a chisel.

Make the rails and stiles, with tenons and mortises, in the usual way, and cut the panel to shape. Set up the tablesaw to cut the bevel, with the blade angled to the correct slope, the height set for the width of the bevel, and the fence placed to the edge thickness of the panel. The straight sides are no problem; just run them through. On the arched top, run the piece through once resting on the top of the arch, then again resting on the top and one corner, and again resting on the top and the other corner.

Now, set the tablesaw to cut the shallow shoulders on the bevels, thus removing the waste from the work. This completes the straight sides, except for cleanup with a rabbet plane, and removes most of the wood from the arched top.

Mark the shoulder line on the arched top and the 45° lines at the changes of direction. Use a wide, sharp chisel to carve the bevel down, making a neat, sharp juncture at the 45° line. Marking the correct thickness on the panel edge and carving back to the shoulder line is one way to do it.

The grooves that accept the panel in the straight sides are easily made with a dado blade in the tablesaw. To make the groove in the top rail, drill holes somewhat smaller than the desired thickness of the groove, then chisel out the groove to the line. Don't worry about the sloppy bottom of the groove, just make the sides nice and even.

Assemble the door dry, pin through the tenons with dowels, and fit it to its opening. Then take it apart and reassemble without the panel to round over the inside edge of the frame with a router. The panel should be finished before glue-up to prevent an unfinished edge from showing through as the door expands and contracts over the years. Make sure the panel is slightly loose on final assembly; that's the whole idea, allowing a little room for expansion and contraction.

—CARY HALL, *Hampton, Ga.*

Copying Cornice Molding on the Tablesaw

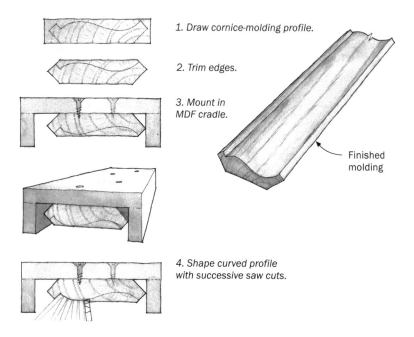

1. Draw cornice-molding profile.

2. Trim edges.

3. Mount in MDF cradle.

Finished molding

4. Shape curved profile with successive saw cuts.

WHILE REMODELING A VICTORIAN-STYLE wood-paneled bath-room, I needed one 5-ft. length of cornice molding to complete the job. After striking out with local suppliers and running up some hefty long-distance phone bills, I found that it would cost about $150 to make the custom knives to run one 5-ft. piece of molding.

Recalling the many times I've cut simple cove moldings on my tablesaw, I had a sudden brainstorm on how to make the cornice in my shop. First, I drew the molding profile on both ends of a blank, a little longer than 5 ft. Then I made two 45° bevel cuts on each edge of the blank to define the top and bottom edges of the molding. Next, I built a cradle of ½-in. medium-density fiberboard (MDF)—a bit longer and slightly wider than the workpiece. I screwed the workpiece to the inside of the cradle, facedown, as shown on the facing page. The cradle eliminates the problems that would result from cutting away the surfaces of the molding if I tried to mill it directly, facedown on the saw.

I made a series of cuts to define the profile, working from both sides of the cradle. For each cut, I tilted the blade to cut as close to 90° to the face of the curve as possible. This makes a cleaner profile and minimizes some of the steps and grooves that have to be scraped and sanded away to complete the shape. After some sanding, I had a cornice molding that was indistinguishable from the original and the satisfaction of proving to myself that it could be done. I also saved $150 to boot.

—Ross M. Greer, *Alexandria, Ont., Canada*

Cutting Concave Bevels on the Tablesaw

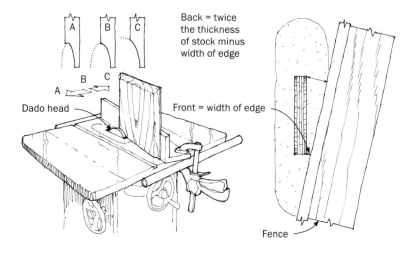

Back = twice the thickness of stock minus width of edge

Dado head

Front = width of edge

Fence

CONCAVE BEVELS ARE SAID TO FIT BETTER into a frame than straight bevels. I have had good results making concave bevels using a modified cove cut on the tablesaw. I run the panel on edge past a dado head using a fence clamped at a slight angle to the blades.

There are several possible profiles when using this approach. I prefer profile B in the drawing, which is produced by setting the blade height to the desired field width and angling the fence according to the instructions shown in the drawing. Moving the fence closer to the rear of the blades will produce profile A, and moving the fence farther from the rear while raising the blades will produce profile C. This cut doesn't usually require a zero-clearance insert. However, a tall fence and a couple of featherboards can greatly enhance the operation.

I usually use a scraper ground to the appropriate curve to clean up the bevel.

—DAVID A. HOOD, *Corvallis, Ore.*

Compound Miters Made Simple

H ERE'S A SIMPLE, FOOLPROOF SOLUTION for finding the proper
blade-tilt and miter-gauge angles for mitering crown molding
on the tablesaw. Set the miter gauge at 45° and the sawblade at 90°.
Crank the blade up to full height. Place a scrap of the molding with
the top face flat against the miter gauge and the bottom edge flat on
the saw table, and make a cut. If the blade cuts all the way through the
molding, go ahead and cut the miters using this setup. With most large
crown moldings, however, you will find that the blade—even at full
height—will not cut through the molding.

If that is the case, you can use the scrap piece as a guide. The cut in
the scrap piece, laid flat on the tablesaw, will show you the needed
blade-tilt and miter-gauge settings. With the saw turned off, tilt the
blade until it just slips into the cut in the scrap piece, then set the
miter gauge to fit snugly against the molding. That's it. No calculations
are required.

—TIM HANSON, *Indianapolis, Ind.*

1. Make cut with blade at
90° and at full height.

2. Lay back of molding on saw
table; use scrap to set blade tilt
and miter-gauge angles.

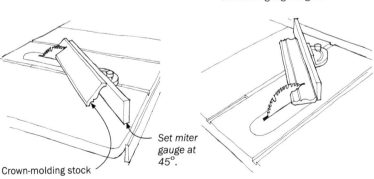

Crown-molding stock

Set miter
gauge at
45°.

Safe Molding on the Tablesaw

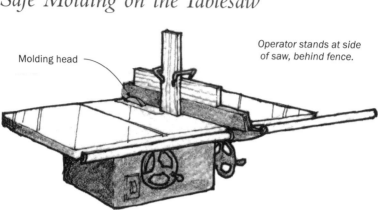

Molding head

Operator stands at side
of saw, behind fence.

A FTER I HAD A $1,300 ACCIDENT at my jointer last year, I have a
renewed interest in safety. The scariest operation I know is using
the molding head on the tablesaw to shape short vertical boards, such
as drawer fronts. I have rendered this operation relatively harmless by
clamping the drawer front to a long board that rides the top of the rip
fence. I guide the work through the blade, standing to one side of the
saw behind the rip fence.

—RICHARD TOLZMAN, *Excelsior, Minn.*

Jig for Making Beveled Notches

F OR A RECENT PRODUCTION RUN OF TOYS, I had to cut several
beveled notches on each toy. My first thought was to use a simple
beveled block attached to my miter gauge that would tilt the workpiece at the appropriate angle for a dado-blade cut. But then I realized
I'd have to try several different angles when building the prototype, re-
quiring many trial-and-error setups. So to save time, I designed the
variable-angle, notch-cutting jig shown in the drawing.

The jig consists of a sliding frame that runs along the miter-gauge
slots in the tables. The frame includes a work-support easel mounted
on a tilt-adjust mechanism. When the easel is set at the desired angle,
the tilt-adjust mechanism clamps it in place.

I adjust the dado blades to the proper height for the desired depth
of cut, and push the whole frame forward to make the cut. I slide the
workpiece to the left or right and make another pass to widen the cut
of the beveled notch.

—JACK HALL, *Newport Beach, Calif.*

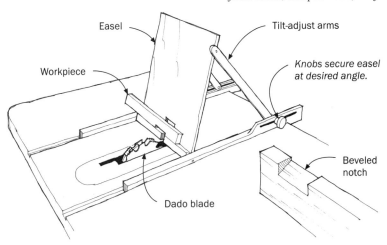

Easel

Tilt-adjust arms

Knobs secure easel
at desired angle.

Workpiece

Beveled
notch

Dado blade

Rounding Over the Edges of Small Boards

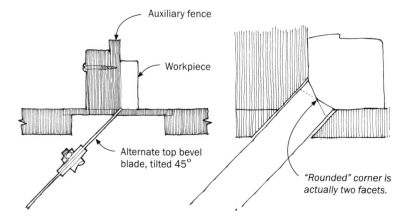

Auxiliary fence

Workpiece

Alternate top bevel
blade, tilted 45°

"Rounded" corner is
actually two facets.

BECAUSE I COULDN'T FIND AN APPROPRIATE router bit for putting a tiny radius on the edges of small boards, I came up with this method using a tablesaw, which cuts a corner that's less than ⅛ in. on a wooden workpiece. First, install a standard alternate top bevel (ATB) sawblade in your tablesaw. ATB blades are fitted with beveled teeth and have no square raker teeth. Set the blade angle to 45°, and use a machinable wooden fence and table insert. Adjust the fence so that the blade's centerline will travel exactly into the square edge of your workpiece. Some eyeballing and trial and error may be required to position the fence. Adjust the radius up to about ⅛ in. by cranking the blade into the edge.

What you are actually getting are two facets along the corner. On this small a scale, the edge looks and feels virtually round, especially if you sand lightly.

—PER MADSEN, *San Francisco, Calif.*

Microgrooves with Masking Tape

WHILE MAKING THE PICTURE-FRAME MOLDING shown in the sketch, I found that I could cut two precise microgrooves simultaneously by using two blades with a spacer between them. To make one of the grooves a tad wider than the normal ⅛-in. kerf, I stuck a small piece of tape on the inside face of the outboard blade to cause it to wobble slightly.

—BRYAN HUMPHREY, *Wilmington, N.C.*

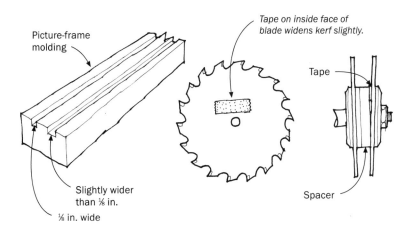

Picture-frame molding

Tape on inside face of blade widens kerf slightly.

Tape

Spacer

Slightly wider than ⅛ in.

⅛ in. wide

Edging Plywood Drawer Fronts

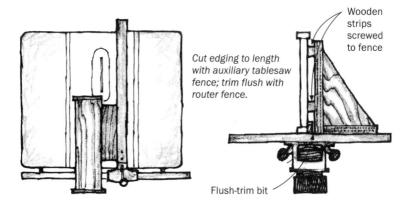

Cut edging to length with auxiliary tablesaw fence; trim flush with router fence.

Wooden strips screwed to fence

Flush-trim bit

HERE ARE A COUPLE OF TRICKS I USE to apply solid-wood edging to plywood drawer fronts. The first is a simple auxiliary tablesaw fence to trim the edging to length. I glue the edging to the ends of the drawer, leaving a ¼-in. overhang. Then, with the auxiliary fence adjusted for a perfect flush cut, I simply push each corner through the saw.

To trim the edging flush with the face of the drawer front, I use the router-table setup shown in the sketch. Make a tall fence for the router table, and screw a couple of wooden strips to it. Chuck a ball-bearing flush-trim bit in the router, and adjust the fence so the bearing is flush with the surface of the strips. When you run the panels through, the edging rides under the bottom strip, and the tall fence makes it easy to keep the panel perpendicular.

—RICK TURNER, *Petaluma, Calif.*

Matching a Box to Its Lid

WHEN I BUILD SMALL BOXES, I construct the box body and the lid together as a solid unit and slice the top away from the box later. This ensures that the lid matches the size and grain of the body perfectly. One word of caution: It's risky to saw the lid right off the box. Instead, set your tablesaw blade's height at ½ in. less than the thickness of the side of the box before sawing all four sides. This approach will leave the lid attached with a thin web of wood, which can be cut with a razor knife before pieces are sanded and finished.

—CURTIS W. MEAD, *Troy, N.H.*

Making Large Pulleys on the Tablesaw

I WAS COMMISSIONED TO BUILD A LARGE, slow-moving turntable as part of a stage set for my community's performing-arts center. It presented a most interesting challenge. The 4-ft. turntable had to be able to hold a 200-lb. actor and spin at 2 rpm. The solution was to use a low-rpm gear-reduction electric motor, further reduced by a V-belt turning a 15-in.-dia. pulley. I had no problem locating the small pulley that fit on the motor shaft. But I was unable to find a 15-in.-dia. pulley locally and did not have a lathe to turn one. However, I found another, very simple method to make the pulley.

The pulley consists of two 15-in.-dia. disks, which I bandsawed from ¾-in.-thick plywood and screwed together. But before assembling the two disks, I used a dado head on the tablesaw to cut an angled rabbet in the edge of each disk to form the groove for the V-belt. To do this, I installed the dado head on my tablesaw and tilted the arbor to the same angle as the side of the V-belt. I clamped a piece of

¼-in.-thick plywood to the top of my saw and drilled a small pivot hole into the plywood, 7½ in. from the dado head and in line with the arbor. Then, with the dado blade lowered, I pushed a pin through the center hole of one of the disks and into the pivot hole in the plywood auxiliary table. Next, I turned the saw on and slowly rotated the plywood disk as I simultaneously slowly raised the dado blade. When the rabbet on the first disk was cut to the proper depth, I lowered the blade, removed the disk and repeated the process with the second disk. I then screwed the two disks together to form a strong, durable pulley with an accurate V-belt groove.

—GENE STEMMANN, *Corvallis, Ore.*

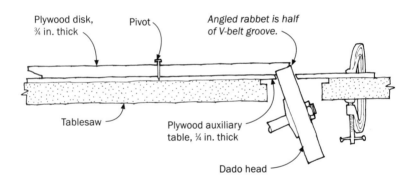

Plywood disk, ¾ in. thick

Pivot

Angled rabbet is half of V-belt groove.

Tablesaw

Plywood auxiliary table, ¼ in. thick

Dado head

Octagon Formulas and Jig

THE SPECIAL JIG AND THE FORMULAS BELOW will enable you to cut an octagon with each side equal to a predetermined length. The jig is a piece of plywood with two fences screwed to the top at 45° to the edge.

To use the jig, first determine the desired length of one side of the finished octagon O. Calculate the square size S needed from the formula $S = 2.414 \times O$, and cut a square S inches on each side. Now, calculate the rip-fence distance R from the formula $R = 2.914 \times O$, and set the rip fence at this distance. Place the square in the jig, and rip off all four corners in turn to produce a perfect octagon.

Example: 3 = desired length of one side of octagon. $S = 2.414 \times 3$, or $S = 7.242$. $R = 2.914 \times 3$, or $R = 8.742$.

—RAFIK ESKANDARIAN, *Fresno, Calif.*

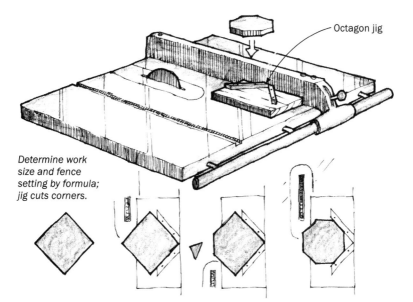

Octagon jig

Determine work size and fence setting by formula; jig cuts corners.

No-Hassle Octagon Ripping

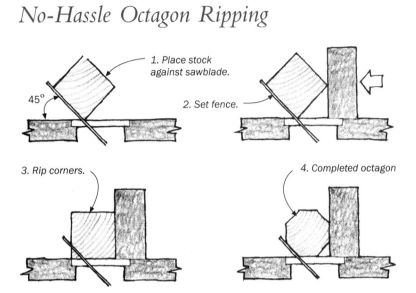

45°

1. Place stock against sawblade.

2. Set fence.

3. Rip corners.

4. Completed octagon

AFTER SPENDING A WEEK MAKING a marking gauge for laying out octagons on stock, I had a flash of inspiration. This method requires no gauge and will allow you to rip perfect octagonal cylinders.

First, determine the size you want the finished octagon to be, then rip your stock to a square. Make a new wooden insert for your tablesaw and, with the saw blade tilted to 45°, bring the blade up through the insert to the maximum depth of cut. Retract the blade to the depth needed to cut the corners off the square stock. A precise kerf line should now be visible fore and aft of the blade in the tablesaw insert.

Now lay your square stock against the blade with the corner of the stock right on the kerf line in the insert. Bring the rip fence up to the stock so that it just touches the corner (as shown in the sketch) and lock. Lay the stock flat on the table against the rip fence, and rip off the corners to produce a perfect octagon.

—L. A. D. COLVIN, *Satellite Beach, Fla.*

Making Louvers

THIS SIMPLE JIG CUTS THE PINS on the ends of the individual louvers in homemade louvered doors. It consists of a V-notched
base, which slides in the tablesaw's miter-gauge track, and a cylindrical
louver holder. A slot in the cylinder holds the louvers in the correct
cutting position, using adjustment and stop screws as shown in the
sketch. To use the jig, load a louver blank into the cylinder, then
tighten a hose clamp around the cylinder to lock the louver in place.
Place the cylinder in the base, push the jig into the blade and rotate
the cylinder to cut a pin on one end of the louver. Remove the louver, reverse it in the cylinder and repeat to cut the other end's pin.

—R. F. PAAKKONEN, *Stafford Springs, Conn.*

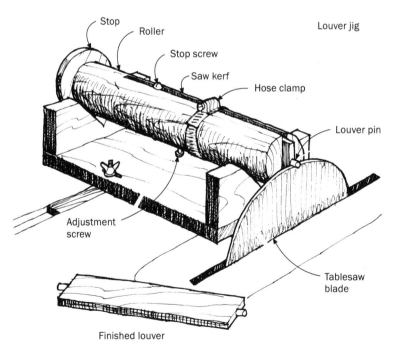

Stop
Roller
Louver jig
Stop screw
Saw kerf
Hose clamp
Louver pin
Adjustment
screw
Tablesaw
blade
Finished louver

Making Dowels with the Tablesaw

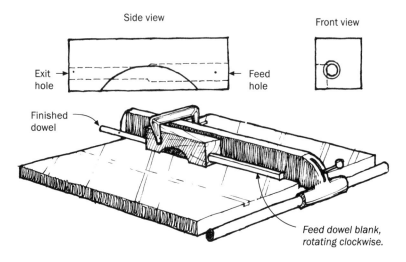

Side view

Front view

Exit hole →

← Feed hole

Finished dowel

Feed dowel blank, rotating clockwise.

I PREFER TO MAKE MY OWN DOWELS, largely because I can then make any-size dowel in any length from any wood. My system is simpler and certainly less expensive than the commercial dowel-making tools that are limited to only a few sizes. The drawings show the complete tooling required: a hardwood block and your tablesaw. The block size isn't critical, but it should be thick enough to clamp easily to the saw's rip fence and long enough to cover the sawblade in use. This last point is important because you'll need to reach across the saw to withdraw the finished dowel.

To construct the fixture, first drill a dowel-sized exit hole through the length of the block. Enlarge this hole from the front, halfway through the block, to produce a feed hole. The diameter of the feed hole should be the same as the diagonal of the square dowel blanks you plan to use. As a guide, the diameter of the feed hole shouldn't exceed the exit hole by ¼ in. Now, clamp the block to the saw's rip fence. Center the block over the blade. In a succession of cove cuts (made by raising the sawblade into the block), cut a channel from the edge to just into the wall of the exit hole. The best blade to use to channel the block and make dowels is a heavy, small-diameter carbide-toothed blade. Next, rip the dowel blanks so they will turn easily in the feed hole. With the block clamped and the fence locked, start the saw and insert the blank. Rotate the blank clockwise, and feed slowly until the blade starts cutting. Adjust the block's position with the rip fence until the dowel fits snugly in the exit hole. It's a good idea to withdraw the dowel and check the size of the first few inches.

In smaller sizes, which are difficult to rotate by hand, I cut a short dowel on one end, then I chuck the short dowel in my portable drill. A slow feed and a slow rotation yield the smoothest dowels.

—LANY CHURCHILL, *Mayville, Wisc.*

Cutting Circles on the Tablesaw

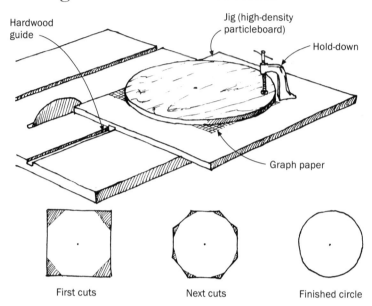

Hardwood guide

Jig (high-density particleboard)

Hold-down

Graph paper

First cuts

Next cuts

Finished circle

OUND TABLETOPS, LAZY-SUSAN SHELVES and other large circles can be cut on the tablesaw with a simple jig. Cut a dado in the underside of a ¾-in. high-density particleboard base and glue in a hardwood key, sized for a sliding fit in the saw's left-hand miter slot. Wax the jig bottom and key to reduce friction. Measuring from the blade, accurately locate and paste sheets of ¼-in. graph paper to the jig top to aid in layout.

To use, first cut the circle blank somewhat oversize and locate its center. Next, mark the radius of the finished circle on the graph paper, and pin the center of the circle blank at this mark. Make sure the blank will rotate freely but is firmly pinned to the jig. Start by lopping off the corners of the blank. Hold the blank and jig firmly while sliding them past the blade. If hand-holding the work appears unsafe, mount a hold-down clamp on the base to lock the blank while cutting. Continue cutting off the corners of the blank until it is almost round. Then, with the work just touching the blade, rotate the blank to trim off all the high spots. The smoothest circles are produced using high-quality, sharp carbide blades.

—PHILIP MARGRAFF, *Coeur d'Alene, Idaho*

Tablesaw Disk Sander from an Old Blade

TO MAKE A REALLY GOOD DISK SANDER, glue coarse and fine disks to an old flat-sided, fine-tooth sawblade, and mount it on the tablesaw's arbor. For safety, use a bench grinder to remove the teeth, then true up on the arbor.

—STAN HAYWOOD, *Sylvan Lake, Alberta, Canada*

Precise Tablesaw Jointer Disk

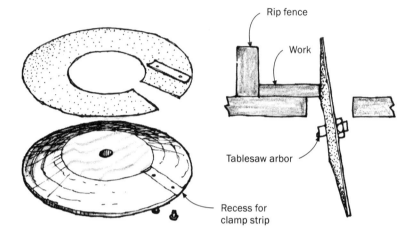

Rip fence

Work

Tablesaw arbor

Recess for
clamp strip

HIS CONE-SHAPED TABLESAW JOINTING DEVICE does precise work,
both in sanding boards to width and in leaving a good gluing
surface. It's basically a 10-in. conical disk made from ¾-in. plywood.
What makes the device special is the small cone angle (9° on mine).
Unlike a flat disk, which contacts the workpiece across its full width,
the cone's contact is restricted to a small area, the radius that's located
directly above the arbor. Another benefit is that vertical adjustments
of the saw arbor produce very small increments in cutting depth. (As
an industrial modelmaker, I sometimes have to work in thousandths
of an inch.)

I fiberglassed the back of my disk for extra strength, and it's served
me well for years. The cutting surface is an abrasive sander disk cut to
fit the cone face and is glued and clamped in place. I use plastic-
laminate glue to secure the paper; to change abrasives, I dissolve the

cement with acetone. Varying the grade of abrasive paper allows various compromises between a fast cutting speed and good surface quality.

To use the sander, tilt the tablesaw's arbor to present a vertical cutting surface, as shown in the drawing. I usually guide the work along the rip fence.

—Dr. Robert Bogle, *La Jolla, Calif.*

Edge-Sanding Fixture

HERE'S A FIXTURE THAT TURNS A BELT SANDER into an edge sander. Simply build a wooden fixture that supports and locks your belt sander in a horizontal position. Bolt the fixture to the tablesaw's rip fence as shown, and use the saw's flat cast-iron surface for the work.

—Wayne Hausknecht, *Tucson, Ariz.*

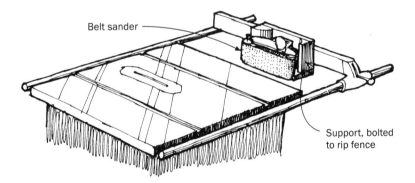

Belt sander

Support, bolted to rip fence

CUTTING
PLYWOOD

Plywood-Scoring Tablesaw Insert

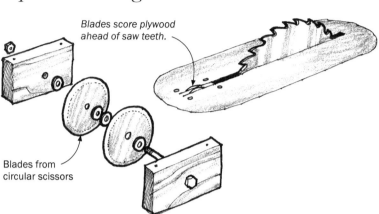

Blades score plywood
ahead of saw teeth.

Blades from
circular scissors

T HIS DEVICE HELPS TO PREVENT the underside of veneered plywood from splintering by scoring the veneer just ahead of the
blade. To make it, cut a snug-fitting insert blank from aluminum or
plywood. Carefully raise the blade through it, and enlarge the slot for
clearance. With a straightedge against the teeth on each side of the
blade, mark the outer edges of the blade's kerf on the front section of
the insert. Cut along these lines with a thin saw to create two slots just
ahead of the blade.

The scoring assembly uses two circular blades from the circular scissors made by Olfa. Spare blades for the scissors are available at sewing
and fabric stores. Make a pillow-block assembly with a bolt axle to attach the scoring blades to the underside of the insert. Use regular
washers, as well as shim washers punched from an aluminum can, to
space the blades on the axle. Bolt the scoring assembly under the insert, making sure it will clear the sawblade and housing when in place.
Ideally, the scorers should make a shallow cut ($\frac{1}{32}$ in. to $\frac{1}{16}$ in.) in the
plywood very slightly wider and in line with the kerf of the blade.

—SANDOR NAGYSZALANCZY, *Santa Cruz, Calif.*

Preventing Splintering when Dadoing Veneered Plywood

TEAROUT OF SURFACE VENEER when dadoing plywood is not unusual, but it can be minimized by paying attention to a few details. Because dadoes aren't often cut very deeply, the power or speed of the cutter isn't usually a problem. The key to clean cutting is the parallel alignment of the cutter to the fence. Any variation from true parallel, either within the stack of dado cutters or to the rip fence, will cause one of the outside blades to catch and tear the thin surface veneer.

To eliminate the splintering, I recommend that you first go back to your standard 10-in. blade, and align your rip fence according to your owner's manual. Make sure that the blade falls dead center in your kerf, and test to see that there is no aftercut as you saw your material. Measure carefully to ensure continuous alignment along the full length of the fence. When stacking your blades and chippers, make sure that there is no foreign matter between the parts and that all surfaces pull up snugly when you tighten the nut. Try a crosscut now, and compare the results. Feed slowly and evenly with good downward pressure on the plywood as it passes the cutter.

A couple of other tricks might also reduce splintering. First, make a wooden throat-plate blank, and raise the dado head through the insert to the desired height. A throat plate cut in this manner will support the delicate veneer fibers right up to the line of the cut. Second, thoroughly burnish a piece of masking tape over the line where the shoulder of the cut will occur. The tape will hold the fibers together while you cut the groove. After the cut, peel the remaining tape away by pulling with the grain, then sand the surface smooth.

—RICH PREISS, *Charlotte, N.C.,*
from a question by Dan Graupensperger, Orange, Calif.

Chip-Free Melamine Cutting

MELAMINE IS A GREAT MATERIAL, but the 4x8 sheets are terribly heavy and the material chips easily. To avoid lifting and moving the heavy panels through a tablesaw, many woodworkers cut them to size with a portable circular saw and a fence clamped across the sheet. If you do use a portable circular saw, however, I would caution you not to expect the best results. A handheld circular saw will simply have too much wobble to give you a really clean cut.

A better strategy would be to rough-cut the panels to a manageable size with your circular saw and then make the finish cuts on the tablesaw.

I've used melamine a great deal. For years, I used a 60-tooth, triple-chip blade to cut it. By slowing down the feed rate, I could get pretty good results, but I still had some noticeable chipout. Then I bought a new blade made especially for melamine and got virtually chip-free cuts. The melamine blade has 80 teeth, an alternate top bevel profile and an extremely steep bevel angle.

—WILLIAM DUCKWORTH,
from a question by Ronald Porter, Ferndale, Wash.

Preventing Chipout by Scoring the Veneer

TO PREVENT CHIPOUT ON EXPENSIVE veneered plywood, first set the sawblade just proud of the table. With the saw turned off, slide the workpiece against the rip fence, pushing down so that it rolls the blade beneath it. Then flip the piece over, clamp on a straightedge, and score the veneer with a knife along the dotted line marked by the tips of the rolling blade.

—LARRY PREUSS, M.D., *Ann Arbor, Mich.*

Plywood Scoring Fixtures

Y OU CAN GREATLY REDUCE the fuzzing and tearout that goes with ripping plywood across the veneer grain by first scoring the lower side of the plywood with a shallow cut of less than ⅛ in. But this requires lowering the blade to make the scoring cut, then raising it again to make the finish cut. These fixtures allow you to make a scoring cut without all this fuss. Just put the two fixtures in place, one against the fence and one near the blade, and push the panel through to make the scoring cut. Then remove the fixtures to make the finish cut. Dowels on the ends of the fixtures prevent them from sliding forward during a cut.

—M. DUGAN, *Bohemia, N.Y.*

Fixtures raise work so blade scores
plywood veneer on first pass.

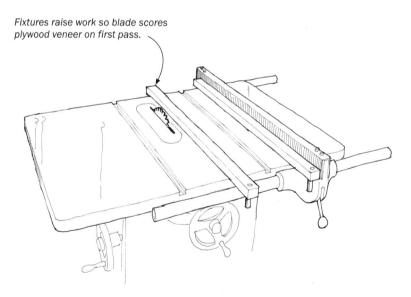

INDEX